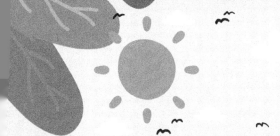

THE ONE BIG BOOK

BIG BOOK

GRADE 7

For English, Math, and Science

★ Includes Math, English, Science - all in one colorful book

★ Detailed instructions to teach and learn with pictures and examples

★ Best book for home schooling, practicing, and teaching

★ Includes answers with detailed explanations

Detailed instructions along with interesting activities

www.aceacademicpublishing.com

Author: Ace Academic Publishing

Prepaze is a sister company of Ace Academic Publishing. Intrigued by the unending possibilities of the internet and its role in education, Prepaze was created to spread the knowledge and learning across all corners of the world through an online platform. We equip ourselves with state-of-the-art technologies so that knowledge reaches the students through the quickest and the most effective channels.

The materials for our books are written by award winning teachers with several years of teaching experience. All our books are aligned with the state standards and are widely used by many schools throughout the country.

For enquiries and bulk order, contact us at the following address:

3736, Fallon Road, #403
Dublin, CA 94568
www.aceacademicpublishing.com

Ace Academic Publishing
ACHIEVING EXCELLENCE TOGETHER

ISBN: 978-1-949383-42-3

Other books from Ace Academic Publishing

 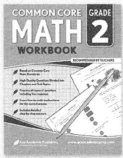 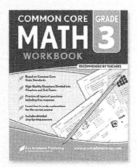 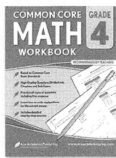 

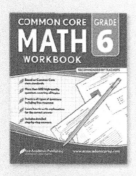  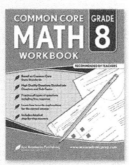  

Ace Academic Publishing
ACHIEVING EXCELLENCE TOGETHER

Other books from Ace Academic Publishing

Ace Academic Publishing

ACHIEVING EXCELLENCE TOGETHER

Contents

English

Math

Science

English

This book enables your children to explore the English language and develop the necessary expertise. A series of thought-provoking exercises, engaging activities, and engrossing puzzles facilitate your children with understanding the intricacies of the English language.

Language

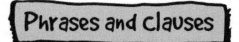

Phrases are groups of words that cannot stand on their own as a sentence. They function as nouns, verbs, prepositions, adjectives, or adverbs in a sentence.

Clauses are groups of words that have a subject and a predicate. Clauses can be dependent, which cannot stand on their own, or independent, which can stand alone.

Different combinations of phrases, dependent clauses, and independent clauses are used together in a sentence to achieve sentences of varied lengths and structure.

Examples

They <u>have been cleaning</u> since morning.
(verb phrase)

The assignments are <u>on the table</u>.
(prepositional phrase)

Unless we achieve our goals, we will not be happy.
——————————————   ———————————————
    dependent clause   independent clause

Identify the Parts

Identify the type of phrase underlined.

1. In the back <u>of the truck</u>, Irene, Adam, and Monica hid the box that they dug up in the morning.

a) Noun phrase   b) Verb phrase   c) Prepositional phrase   d) Infinitive phrase

2. I did not disturb them even though they <u>had been sleeping</u> for hours.

a) Noun phrase   b) Verb phrase   c) Prepositional phrase   d) Infinitive phrase

3. Before the parade, they <u>will have finished decorating</u> the float and truck.

a) Noun phrase   b) Verb phrase   c) Prepositional phrase   d) Infinitive phrase

4. Elliot forgot his friend's birthday, and when he finally remembered, he sent him <u>a handmade gift</u>.

a) Noun phrase   b) Verb phrase   c) Prepositional phrase   d) Infinitive phrase

5. After consulting with my family, I agreed <u>to take</u> the offer.

a) Noun phrase   b) Verb phrase   c) Prepositional phrase   d) Infinitive phrase

prepaze

Read the instructions and answer accordingly.

1. Circle the phrase that modifies the noun "girl."

The girl with the ponytail is walking toward the podium.

2. Circle the verb phrase that indicates the action in the sentence.

Even before the tests, the patients may take precautionary measures and avoid outdoors.

3. Circle a noun phrase (a group of words that can act as a subject or an object) in the sentence.

The investigators enquired one of our neighbors about their stolen car.

4. Circle the phrase that modifies the verb "welcomed."

The student council welcomed the teachers with great enthusiasm.

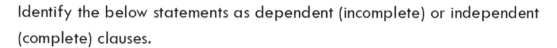 

Complete or Incomplete?

Identify the below statements as dependent (incomplete) or independent (complete) clauses.

1. He informed the hotel staff that the shower head was clogged.

a) complete

b) incomplete

2. Than her father can ever teach the dance moves.

a) complete

b) incomplete

3. Until I call, stay in the attic.

a) complete

b) incomplete

4. According to me, a park is a perfect place for people watching, and a mall is a perfect place for spending time with friends.

a) complete

b) incomplete

5. When the parents or legal guardians of these courageous and persistent children arrive.

a) complete

b) incomplete

6. Identified the technical errors in the research paper and documented the changes.

a) complete

b) incomplete

7. No matter how the scientists approach this problem, they end up at the same point.

a) complete

b) incomplete

8. As the rationale for dividing the funds eludes the committee.

a) complete

b) incomplete

Identify the underlined parts as a phrase or clause. Circle the correct choice, and explain why it is a phrase / clause.

1. The people organized <u>a search party</u> to find the missing dog.

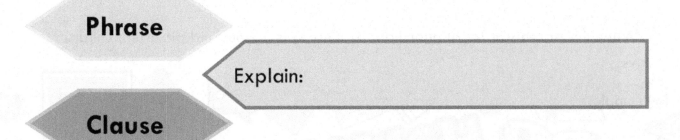

Phrase

Explain:

Clause

2. <u>As the winning team received the award</u>, the fans cheered and chanted in support.

Phrase

Clause

Explain:

3. A few of the students, <u>who supported the cause</u>, gathered for the rally.

Phrase

Clause

Explain:

4. <u>Many of the volunteers</u> were awarded a ribbon as a token of appreciation.

Phrase

Clause

Explain:

5. The gym is ready to operate to its full capacity <u>as the parents worked ceaselessly</u> to install the equipment.

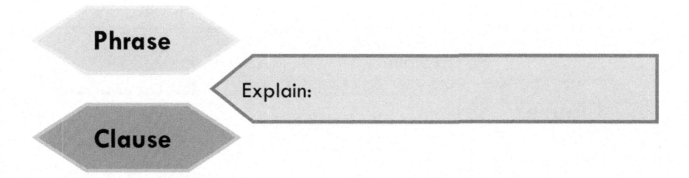

Phrase

Explain:

Clause

6. Although the lecture was long, <u>the students enjoyed it.</u>

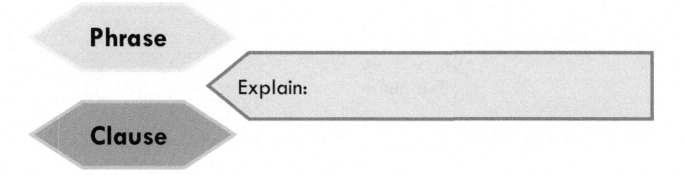

Phrase

Explain:

Clause

Sentence Structure

There are four main types of sentence structure:

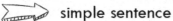 simple sentence

 compound sentence

complex sentence

compound-complex sentence

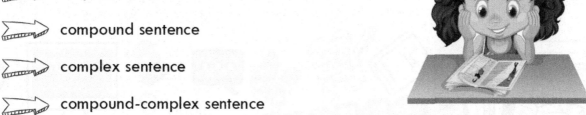

Using sentences of varied lengths and structure reflects an adept writing style.

Examples

Simple Sentence

1 Independent Clause

↓

<u>They ran.</u>

Complex Sentence

1 Dependent Clause + 1 Independent Clause

↓ ↓

<u>Although they ran,</u> <u>they missed the bus.</u>

Compound Sentence

1 Independent Clause + (conjunction/semicolon) + 1 Independent Clause

↓ ↓ ↓

<u>They ran,</u> <u>yet</u> <u>they missed the bus.</u>

Compound-Complex Sentence

1 Dependent Clause + 1 Independent Clause + 1 Independent Clause

↓ ↓ ↓

<u>Although they ran,</u> <u>they missed the bus,</u> and <u>they were late.</u>

prepaze

Find the Structure

Determine the sentence structure of the following.

1. Before you leave, could you please water the plants?

- ○ simple sentence
- ○ compound sentence
- ○ complex sentence
- ○ compound-complex sentence

2. Children enrolled in the vocational and extracurricular activities must pass the tests and practicals.

- ○ simple sentence
- ○ compound sentence
- ○ complex sentence
- ○ compound-complex sentence

3. My father asked me to take the dog for a walk after I completed my homework.

- ○ simple sentence
- ○ compound sentence
- ○ complex sentence
- ○ compound-complex sentence

4. We enjoyed the comedy movie, and we decided to watch it again even though it was not what we expected.

○ simple sentence

○ compound sentence

○ complex sentence

○ compound-complex sentence

5. They lost the GPS signal en route, but they managed to reach the destination.

○ simple sentence

○ compound sentence

○ complex sentence

○ compound-complex sentence

6. Prior to the storm, an amber alert was issued by the government to warn the residents.

○ simple sentence

○ compound sentence

○ complex sentence

○ compound-complex sentence

Transform Me

Change the following sentences as directed.

Example

Convert the given sentence into a complex sentence.

<u>Compound:</u> They ran, yet they missed the bus.

Complex(answer): <u>Although</u> they ran, they missed the bus.

---

1. Convert the given sentences into a compound sentence.

   Sam met with an accident. He was unharmed.

2. Transform the given sentence into an independent clause.

   After considering the consequences.

3. Convert the given sentences into a complex sentence.

   The pizza was cold. We warmed it in the microwave.

4. Convert the given sentence into a simple sentence.

After the game, the players were tired. They needed rest.

Misplaced and Dangling Modifiers

A modifier in a sentence modifies another word or word group. When the modifier is placed far from the word it modifies, it is called a **misplaced modifier.**

A modifier that is incorrectly used to describe something that is not given (absent) in a sentence results in a **dangling modifier.**

These errors in modifiers make it difficult for the readers to understand the text.

Examples

Misplaced modifier

<u>Incorrect:</u> The girl was reported to the principal with long hair.

This sentence means that the principal had long hair.

<u>Correct:</u> The girl <u>with long hair</u> was reported to the principal.

Here, the modifier "with long hair" is placed close to the word it is intended to modify "girl."

Dangling modifier

<u>Incorrect:</u> While packing hastily, the sock fell out of the bag.

This sentence sounds like the sock was packing. Providing a subject can fix it.

<u>Correct:</u> While **he** was packing hastily, the sock fell out of the bag.

Is This Correct?

Select the sentences that are correct.

1. a) The boy walked toward the door carrying his dog.

   b) The boy carrying his dog walked toward the door.

2. a) Leaning against the tree, the farmer's son was hit by a coconut.

   b) Leaning against the tree, a coconut hit the farmer's son.

3. a) Working throughout the weekend, the assignment was completed in time.

   b) Working throughout the weekend, they completed the assignment in time.

Fix Me!

Rewrite the below sentences by replacing the modifiers next to the words they modify.

Piled up in the corner, I removed the trash.

The Bunny Club almost sold all the cookies at the bake sale.

Rewrite the below sentences by providing appropriate subject for the dangling modifiers.

Looking at the sky, ideas came pouring in.

Using the theory of relativity, the behavior of objects was explained.

A comma is used mainly to indicate a pause or separate items in a sentence.

Examples

Here are a few rules and examples for using commas:

 between words in a series or a list

Please bring an easel, a tablet, paint, and two brushes.

 between two or more adjectives of the same adjective group

We noticed huge red, white, and blue flags around the hotel.

after an introductory word/phrase/clauses

Before the game, the players received a pep talk from their coach.

 after a dependent clause

Since we have limited storage space, we avoid bulk ordering.

 before the coordinating conjunction that combines two independent clauses

The marathon was organized by one of the biggest establishments in the city, and it benefited many charities.

 before and after appositives

Mr. Wilson, who volunteered, spent five hours every week for the program.

Read the following sentences, and add commas between the coordinating adjectives.

Please welcome the lovely brilliant and talented performer.

It was a bright sunny day when we reached Ohio.

Her crisp declamatory grandiloquent speech left the audience in awe.

This dish has Persian Arabic and Afghani influences.

The angry callous bird pecked at the windows.

Which one Is correct?

Choose the sentence that uses commas correctly.

1. a) The lion, carefully, guided her cub across the river and the photographer captured the precious moment without their knowledge.

b) The lion carefully guided her cub across the river, and the photographer captured the precious, moment without their knowledge.

c) The lion carefully, guided her cub across the river, and the photographer captured the precious moment without their knowledge.

d) The lion carefully guided her cub across the river, and the photographer captured the precious moment without their knowledge.

2. a) Pamella bought a car, refrigerator and washing machine for her parents.

b) Pamella bought a car, refrigerator, and washing machine for, her, parents.

c) Pamella bought a car, refrigerator, and washing machine for her parents.

d) Pamella bought a car, refrigerator, and washing machine for her, parents.

3. a) March 14 2008, is the most important day of my life, as I was born on that day.

b) March, 14, 2008 is the most important day of my life as I was born on that day.

c) March 14, 2008, is the most important day of my life, as I was born on that day.

d) March 14, 2008, is the most important day of my life as I was born on that day.

4. a) After the test the children, anxiously, waited for the results.

b) After the test, the children anxiously waited for the results.

c) After the test the children anxiously waited, for the results.

d) After the test, the children, anxiously waited for the results.

5. a) I babysit a couple of lovely, adorable, enthusiastic children on weekends.

b) I babysit a couple of lovely, adorable, enthusiastic, children on weekends.

c) I babysit a couple of lovely, adorable enthusiastic children, on weekends.

d) I babysit a couple of lovely adorable enthusiastic children, on weekends.

6. a) My father who is a paleontologist took Stephanie, Irene, Andrew and me to the museum.

b) My father, who is a paleontologist, took Stephanie, Irene, Andrew and me to the museum.

c) My father, who is a paleontologist, took Stephanie, Irene, Andrew, and me to the museum.

d) My father, who is a paleontologist took Stephanie, Irene, Andrew, and me to the museum.

Spelling

English has a vast amount of vocabulary that makes it difficult for an average person to know all the words. Also, spelling can be challenging due to many factors such as conjugation, affixes, loanwords, homonyms, and multiple words to express the same idea.

Spelling can be improved by identifying a pattern in the errors we make and practising to avoid those patterns.

Examples

The following are a couple of common patterns:

Confusion between "ie" and "ei": mischievous, foreign

Often times, we are confused if it is "a" "o" or "e" before the final "r": grammar, cemetery

Try to find patterns in your writing while you edit your work.

Circle the correct spelling of the word.

1. We agreed that calculating the market risk is a _____ to the final step of this project.

a) precursor   b) precurser

2. The pandemic proved to be a _____ blow to our economy.

a) grievous   b) greivous

3. His hair was wet and _____ .

a) dishevelled   b) disheveled

4. She is often mistaken to be _____ and lazy.

a) feckless   b) feckles

5. My mom is an honest and _____ person.

a) guilless   b) guileless

Connect Sentences

Put a checkmark across the words that are correctly spelled, and rewrite the correct spelling for misspelled words.

Words	Correct Spelling
indispensible	
millennium	
accidently	
consceintious	
inoculate	
flourescent	
resucsitation	
venaration	
minuscule	
allegience	

Wordiness

Competitive tests and contemporary readers require us to be precise in our writing. Also, wordiness indirectly indicates lack of ideas or words. Redundancy is a category of wordiness.

Example

Wordy: In my own personal opinion, we should tarp the furniture and floor.

The phrase at the beginning of the sentence is wordy and unnecessary.

Revision: I believe we should tarp the furniture and floor.

Fix the wordy sentences by removing redundant and unnecessary words.

1. The lasagna was really extremely delicious.

prepaze

2. All things considered, the cities are cleaner than ever before.

3. She took the job on account of the fact that it was necessary for her to pay her tuition fee.

4. The pipelines were connected together.

5. We came to a mutual agreement that we will share the cottage.

context clues

Context clues are information or hints found around a word or phrase to suggest its meaning.

Example

Tommy is one of the popular boys in my school, and we gave him the sobriquet "Mr. Popular."

Not many may know the meaning of the word "sobriquet," but looking at the context "popular boy" "gave" "Mr. Popular," we can guess the word means nickname.

Use the context

Find the meaning of the underlined words using the context.

1. I trusted my best friend to always speak the truth, but I was shocked by her <u>mendacity</u>.

a) genuineness

b) untruthfulness

c) authenticity

2. Though the surgery was done in time, her condition <u>deteriorated</u>.

a) degenerated

b) dematerialized

c) defenestrated

3. The new house we moved in is <u>reminiscent</u> of memories of my childhood home.

a) provide sufficient details

b) deliver goods to a destination

c) remind one of something

4. My neighbor is a classic example of a <u>narcissist</u>; he cannot think or talk about anything other than himself.

a) self-righteous

b) self-centered

c) selfless

5. They are a <u>complaisant</u> host who take care of all our requests and demands.

a) unobliging

b) eradicating

c) accommodating

Find the clue

Identify the meaning of the underlined words. Then, in the box, explain the clue words that aided in finding the meaning.

1. The critics <u>postulate</u> that a text reveals the thought process of a writer. This explanation was convincing as most of my writing reflects my thoughts.

a) criticize

b) claim

b) eliminate

[ ]

2. She spent the entire afternoon <u>meandering</u> around the streets instead of sitting at home.

a) wander aimlessly

b) unweave naturally

b) disguise stealthily

[ ]

prepaze

Root Words and Affixes

Root words are words to which affixes can be added to create new words. Some root words can stand alone, and some may not.

Example

Let's take the Latin root **bell** and add affixes to it.

Root: bell (means war or fighting)

Prefix: rebel (means a person who opposes or fights against someone)

Suffix: rebellion (means an act of opposing)

prepaze

Match the Meaning

Match the words with their meaning using your knowledge of root words.

belligerent   different

philanthropy   engraving

heteronym   interrupt

inscription   generosity

disrupt   hostile

Missing Boxes

The word mono is a Greek root which means one.

Use the clues in the below table and complete the missing boxes highlighted in green.

Roots	Suffixes	Words	Meaning
mono		monochrome	a single hue
mono	logue		
mono	poly		exclusive control of a product or service
mono	phonic		
mono		monotony	one tone
mono			a ruler
mono			single eyeglass

Reference Materials

Reference materials come handy when in doubt or when you research for facts. Reference materials can be found in print and digital media.

The most popularly used reference material is a dictionary.

Example

A typical dictionary includes the following:

⟹ headword (the word you look up)

⟹ the syllable break up

⟹ pronunciation

⟹ part of speech

⟹ meaning

⟹ usage in phrase/sentence

prepaze

Look It Up

Refer to a dictionary and write the part of speech and meaning of the following words. Then, write a new sentence using the word.

	Part of speech	Meaning
Ambivalence		
Sentence		
Condone		
Sentence		
Plausible		
Sentence		
Subordinate		
Sentence		
Ubiquitous		
Sentence		
Viability		
Sentence		

prepaze

Spot the odd one

Use a reference material to find the answer. Circle the odd one.

1. All but one are nouns

Dog   Carrot   Cat

Arrive   Flask

2. All but one are adjectives

Exactly   Beautiful   Dark

Short   Tall

3. All but one are conjunctions

And   But   Although

Flame   Because

4. All but one are adverbs

Quickly   Almost   Simply

Scruffy   Yesterday

5. All but one are verbs

Write   Consider   Sleep

Kind   Hesitate

prepaze

Allusion

Allusion is an indirect reference to someone or something from mythological, literary, historical, or biblical significance. The reader is expected to understand the reference without much explanation.

Example

We were surprised that his nose did not grow after all the lies he had been saying.

Did you catch the allusion here?

The words "nose did not grow" alludes to Pinocchio from the story *The Adventures of Pinocchio*. In the story, Pinocchio's nose grows with every lie he tells. This is an example of a **literary** allusion.

Identify the Allusion

Choose the best description for the underlined allusions.

1. Don't be a <u>Scrooge</u> during the holiday season, Martin!

a) greedy and unkind

b) generous and sympathetic

c) lavish and resourceful

2. Getting these two to get along is harder than <u>getting a camel through the eye of a needle</u>.

a) possible situation

b) a situation that requires effort

c) impossible situation

3. She gave everything she had for this job, but the new manager proved to be her <u>nemesis</u>.

a) someone who supports sincerely

b) someone who acts indifferently

c) someone who cannot be conquered

4. He is no <u>Einstein</u>, but he can be very charming and persuasive.

a) studious

b) genius

c) ignorant

5. My brothers are very protective and <u>Argus-eyed</u> about me.

a) moribund

b) negligent

c) vigilant

Find the Allusion

Underline the allusions in the below statements and explain your answer in the box below.

1. The government believed that it could cut through the Gordian knot of the imploding economy.

2. She exclaimed, "Please stop acting like a Romeo."

3. This resort looks like the Garden of Eden. I could live here forever.

4. With a Herculean effort, the workers lifted the concrete pillar to free the boy trapped underneath.

5. To us nationalists, he is the Judas.

Make Allusions

Write three allusions using prior knowledge of history, literature, religion, or mythology.

Word Analogy

An analogy is used to compare two things that are otherwise unlike. There are different types of word analogies.

Examples

Do you find any similarity between a finger and a leaf? Look at the below example.

finger : human :: leaf : _____

a) branch   b) tree   c) stem   d) root

We know that the finger is a part of a human. Since leaf is the first word in the second pair, we know that it, too, is the part of a whole. Branch, stem, and root are also parts of a tree. Therefore, to match the analogy in the first pair, the best word to go in the blanks is "tree."

Try completing the below analogy.

finger : hand :: leaf : _____

a) branch   b) tree   c) stem   d) root

In this analogy, the finger is to hand (which itself is a part of a human) as leaf is to stem (which is a part of a tree).

Connect the Analogies

Match the word pairs on the left to the pairs on the right that share the same relationship.

waitress : restaurant	docile : compliant
pebble : boulder	mahogany : timber
anaconda : snake	shoal : fish
gallant : valiant	awkward : relaxed
troupe : dancers	pond: sea
polite : rude	lawyer : courtroom

Find the Matching Pair

Choose the word pair that shares the same relationship as the given pair.

1. doctor : nurse

a) skeleton : femur

b) businessman : secretary

c) audiologist : patient

d) none of the above

2. pressure : Pascal

a) relativity : Einstein

b) temperature : Farenheit

c) area : Newton

d) none of the above

4. medicine : dispensary

a) trousers : garment

b) chisel : carve

c) bees : apiary

d) none of the above

3. choreographer : Tango

a) reading : knowledge

b) jewelry : gold

c) dramatist : play

d) none of the above

5. cockroach : nymph

a) swan : cygnet

b) fox : vixen

c) frog : amphibian

d) none of the above

prepaze

Write Analogy

Identify the relationship between the given pair of words and write a similar word pair to complete the analogy.

1. asphalt : road

2. scientist : laboratory

3. race : track

Riddle

Complete the analogy.

YSM : MIE :: NHB : ?

Synonyms and Antonyms

Synonyms are words that share the same or similar meaning. Antonyms are words that share the opposite meaning.

Examples

Jenna is a <u>voracious</u> reader.

Jenna is a <u>compulsive</u> reader.

The words voracious and compulsive both mean insatiable or wanting more.

These math problems appear to be <u>complex</u>; we need to find a <u>simple</u> approach to solve them.

The words complex and simple are antonyms.

Spot the odd one

In each row, circle the word that is not a synonym.

1	enraged	vehement	introvert	furious
2	apprise	endeavor	notify	announce
3	profound	indigenous	sincere	unfeigned
4	tedious	unvarying	accolade	monotonous
5	orthodox	embezzle	traditional	conservative
6	apprehensive	frightened	anxious	vigorous
7	segment	permeate	fraction	component
8	garrulous	abate	subside	diminish

Find the Match

Match the synonyms and shade them with the same color.

1.	mischievous		descend
2.	answer		waste
3.	create		playful
4.	hurry		correct
5.	ruin		chilly
6.	drop		develop
7.	accurate		respond
8.	cold		rush

Match the antonyms.

feasible	appease
astute	impracticable
disheveled	ingnorance
erratic	witless
cognizance	orderly
exasperate	predictable

prepaze

Word Puzzle

Circle the synonyms of the below words in the word search, and write the answers in the correct boxes.

1. plan

2. wreck

3. expand

4. expose

5. obtain

6. silent

```
              K T
            T Y B M
          S A F S S N
        B G X S P R T E
        R S Y X V H B Q D U
      U K T T Y F Y B Y S G L
    E O K R E S C A R E P P O F
  L N W E O I F A R J I W Q I Y Y
K X U H N N U E O M T Q R L N Q R A
Z A X F Z U G Q B J E I W X P N X R R A
F R E T T A H S P U S P E N D E D U F D
  I I D J O M N M Y A P L D I K A H Y
    P V Y I F N P V R E V E A L R P
      B F Z E R I U Q C A S R J O
        J D E S I G N K Q F M R
          J F H W G F H Q S H
            P Z X S M C M F
              V E R Y M P
                X I N N
                  I S
```

Connotation and Denotation

In English, some words share the same literal/denotative meaning, but connote different emotions or ideas.

Example

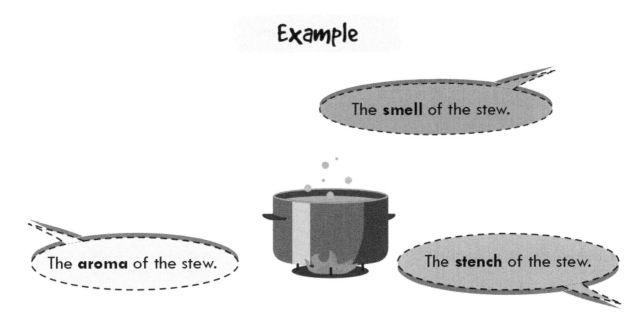

The **smell** of the stew.

The **aroma** of the stew.

The **stench** of the stew.

Here, the words smell, aroma, and stench all indicate the scent of the stew.

However, the word **aroma** has a **positive connotation**, and the word **stench** has a **negative connotation**. The word **smell** is neutral.

Choose the words/phrases with positive connotation to complete the sentences.

1. He budgets his expenses. He is _____.

a) stingy

b) economical

2. She is _____ .

a) easygoing

b) indifferent

3. His writings reflect his _____ mind.

a) prying

b) inquisitive

Choose the words/phrases with negative connotation to complete the sentences.

1. They like _____ .

a) studying others' work

b) scrutinizing other's work

2. He _____ any situation to his advantage.

a) uses

b) exploits

3. The observation revealed that group A participants were _____ .

a) wilful

b) resolute

prepaze

Each set of words connote positive, negative, and neutral meanings. Match them.

1.

Neutral	Confident
Positive	Egotistical
Negative	secure

2.

Neutral	Jabbering
Positive	Chatty
Negative	Conversational

Reading: Literature

Read the story by Hans Christian Andersen and answer the questions that follow.

Many, many years ago lived an emperor, who thought so much of new clothes that he spent all his money in order to obtain them; his only ambition was to be always well dressed. He did not care for his soldiers, and the theatre did not amuse him; the only thing, in fact, he thought anything of was to drive out and show a new suit of clothes. He had a coat for every hour of the day; and as one would say of a king "He is in his cabinet," so one could say of him, "The emperor is in his dressing-room."

The great city where he resided was very gay; every day many strangers from all parts of the globe arrived. One day two swindlers[1] came to this city; they made people believe that they were weavers, and declared they could manufacture the finest cloth to be imagined. Their colours and patterns, they said, were not only exceptionally beautiful, but the clothes made of their material possessed the wonderful quality of being invisible to any man who was unfit for his office or unpardonably stupid.

"That must be wonderful cloth," thought the emperor. "If I were to be dressed in a suit made of this cloth I should be able to find out which men in my empire were unfit for their places, and I could distinguish the clever from the stupid. I must have this cloth woven for me without delay." And he gave a large sum of money to the swindlers, in advance, that they should set to work without any loss of time. They set up two looms, and pretended to be very hard at work, but they did nothing whatever on the looms. They asked for the finest silk and the most precious gold-cloth; all they got they did away with, and worked at the empty looms till late at night.

"I should very much like to know how they are getting on with the cloth," thought the emperor. But he felt rather uneasy when he remembered that he who was not fit for his office could not see it. Personally, he was of opinion that he had nothing to fear, yet he thought it advisable to send somebody else first to see how matters stood. Everybody in the town knew what a remarkable quality the stuff possessed, and all were anxious to see how bad or stupid their neighbours were.

"I shall send my honest old minister to the weavers," thought the emperor. "He can judge best how the stuff looks, for he is intelligent, and nobody understands his office better than he."

The good old minister went into the room where the swindlers sat before the empty looms. "Heaven preserve us!" he thought, and opened his eyes wide, "I cannot see anything at all," but he did not say so. Both swindlers requested him to come near, and asked him if he did not admire the exquisite pattern and the beautiful colours, pointing to the empty looms. The poor old minister tried his very best, but he could see nothing, for

there was nothing to be seen. "Oh dear," he thought, "can I be so stupid? I should never have thought so, and nobody must know it! Is it possible that I am not fit for my office? No, no, I cannot say that I was unable to see the cloth."

"Now, have you got nothing to say?" said one of the swindlers, while he pretended to be busily weaving.

"Oh, it is very pretty, exceedingly beautiful," replied the old minister looking through his glasses. "What a beautiful pattern, what brilliant colours! I shall tell the emperor that I like the cloth very much."

"We are pleased to hear that," said the two weavers, and described to him the colours and explained the curious pattern. The old minister listened attentively, that he might relate to the emperor what they said; and so he did.

Now the swindlers asked for more money, silk and gold-cloth, which they required for weaving. They kept everything for themselves, and not a thread came near the loom, but they continued, as hitherto[2], to work at the empty looms.

Soon afterwards the emperor sent another honest courtier[3] to the weavers to see how they were getting on, and if the cloth was nearly finished. Like the old minister, he looked and looked but could see nothing, as there was nothing to be seen.

"Is it not a beautiful piece of cloth?" asked the two swindlers, showing and explaining the magnificent pattern, which, however, did not exist.

"I am not stupid," said the man. "It is therefore my good appointment for which I am not fit. It is very strange, but I must not let any one know it;" and he praised the cloth, which he did not see, and expressed his joy at the beautiful colours and the fine pattern. "It is very excellent," he said to the emperor.

Everybody in the whole town talked about the precious cloth. At last the emperor wished to see it himself, while it was still on the loom. With a number of courtiers, including the two who had already been there, he went to the two clever swindlers, who now worked as hard as they could, but without using any thread.

"Is it not magnificent?" said the two old statesmen who had been there before. "Your Majesty must admire the colours and the pattern." And then they pointed to the empty looms, for they imagined the others could see the cloth.

"What is this?" thought the emperor, "I do not see anything at all. That is terrible! Am I stupid? Am I unfit to be emperor? That would indeed be the most dreadful thing that could happen to me."

prepaze

"Really," he said, turning to the weavers, "your cloth has our most gracious approval;" and nodding contentedly he looked at the empty loom, for he did not like to say that he saw nothing. All his attendants, who were with him, looked and looked, and although they could not see anything more than the others, they said, like the emperor, "It is very beautiful." And all advised him to wear the new magnificent clothes at a great procession[4] which was soon to take place. "It is magnificent, beautiful, excellent," one heard them say; everybody seemed to be delighted, and the emperor appointed the two swindlers "Imperial Court weavers."

The whole night previous to the day on which the procession was to take place, the swindlers pretended to work, and burned more than sixteen candles. People should see that they were busy to finish the emperor's new suit. They pretended to take the cloth from the loom, and worked about in the air with big scissors, and sewed with needles without thread, and said at last: "The emperor's new suit is ready now."

The emperor and all his barons then came to the hall; the swindlers held their arms up as if they held something in their hands and said: "These are the trousers!" "This is the coat!" and "Here is the cloak!" and so on. "They are all as light as a cobweb, and one must feel as if one had nothing at all upon the body; but that is just the beauty of them."

"Indeed!" said all the courtiers; but they could not see anything, for there was nothing to be seen.

"Does it please your Majesty now to graciously undress," said the swindlers, "that we may assist your Majesty in putting on the new suit before the large looking-glass?"

The emperor undressed, and the swindlers pretended to put the new suit upon him, one piece after another; and the emperor looked at himself in the glass from every side.

"How well they look! How well they fit!" said all. "What a beautiful pattern! What fine colours! That is a magnificent suit of clothes!"

The master of the ceremonies announced that the bearers of the canopy, which was to be carried in the procession, were ready.

"I am ready," said the emperor. "Does not my suit fit me marvellously?" Then he turned once more to the looking-glass, that people should think he admired his garments.

The chamberlains[5], who were to carry the train, stretched their hands to the ground as if they lifted up a train, and pretended to hold something in their hands; they did not like people to know that they could not see anything.

The emperor marched in the procession under the beautiful canopy, and all who saw him in the street and out of the windows exclaimed: "Indeed, the emperor's new suit is incomparable!

What a long train he has! How well it fits him!" Nobody wished to let others know he saw nothing, for then he would have been unfit for his office or too stupid. Never emperor's clothes were more admired.

"But he has nothing on at all," said a little child at last. "Good heavens! listen to the voice of an innocent child," said the father, and one whispered to the other what the child had said. "But he has nothing on at all," cried at last the whole people. That made a deep impression upon the emperor, for it seemed to him that they were right; but he thought to himself, "Now I must bear up to the end." And the chamberlains walked with still greater dignity, as if they carried the train which did not exist.

---

[1] swindlers: fraud; [2] hitherto: until now; [3] courtier: an adviser in a royal court;

[4] procession: a number of people and vehicle moving together;

[5] chamberlains: a person in charge of a royal household

Story Elements

1. Why would one say of the emperor as "The emperor is in his dressing-room"?

a) He is amused by the art of making clothes and promotes it.

b) His cabinet is adjacent to the dressing-room.

c) He is often found in the dressing-room trying on new clothes

2. Which of the following words aptly describes the emperor?

a) Courageous

b) Vain

c) Humble

3. Which of the following words aptly describes the courtiers?

a) Oblivious

b) Obsequious

c) Assertive

4. Which of the following statements is **true** of the swindlers?

a) They were residents of the emperor's city.

b) They manufactured the finest cloth to be imagined.

c) They appeared to work hard at the empty looms.

5. Which of these statements is **false**?

a) The emperor knew from the beginning that he was tricked by the swindlers.

b) The emperor trusted his courtiers and chamberlains.

c) The emperor paid the swindlers in advance and gave them whatever they asked for to make the suit.

6. What is the tone of the author in this sentence?

"Is it not a beautiful piece of cloth?" asked the two swindlers, showing and explaining the magnificent pattern.

a) Serious

b) Indifferent

c) Humourous

7. Which of these statements show how people in the story think?

a) They confront people who follow absurd things and make them understand that it is not the right thing to do.

b) People force others to believe what they believe in with the help of violence.

c) They follow something that they know is absurd just because people around them believe it is the right thing to do.

8. In current times, how is the moral of the story relatable to us?

a) We should not be vain about our looks.

b) We should not blindly follow fashion trends or follow a crowd without knowing the facts.

c) We should not be obedient to the authority even if the authority is righteous.

9. What is the theme of this story?

a) Chaos and order

b) Pride and vanity

c) Beauty of simplicity

10. Why did the emperor continue the procession even after realizing he was wearing nothing?

a) He was too ashamed to confront his people.

b) He was too foolish to realize he was not wearing anything.

c) He was too proud to accept his gullibility.

 Did You Know?

The idiom "emperor's new clothes" originated from this story.

It is used to imply how humans follow what everyone else around them follows without questioning its authenticity. Sometimes, people know something is not sensible, and yet they go with the popular opinion.

Idioms

Find the meaning of the below idioms.

1. It looked impossible to complete the trail and reach the top of the falls, but we wanted to go <u>the whole nine yards</u>.

What does the underlined idiom mean?

a. all the way

b. nine percent of the determined measure

c. to a measurable extent

2. I was too smart to let them <u>pull the wool over my eyes</u>.

What does the idiom "to pull the wool over somebody's eyes" mean?

a. to acquire inconsequential amount of knowledge

b. to become an accomplice

c. to deceive someone

3. The cousins are like <u>two peas in a pod</u>. What does the underlined idiom mean?

a) always different

b) overconfident

c) very similar

prepaze

Decode the Word

The sentences describe the duties of various professions mentioned in the passage. Identify the profession using the clues and solve the word.

a king or a ruler

a person whose job is weaving fabric

a person who attends a royal court or is an adviser

a person who attends to the needs of a ruler

a person engaged in military services

a person in charge of a royal household

resilence to cope with duties and difficulties

Mending Wall

By Robert Frost

Something there is that doesn't love a wall,

That sends the frozen-ground-swell under it,

And spills the upper boulders in the sun;

And makes gaps even two can pass abreast.

The work of hunters is another thing:

I have come after them and made repair

Where they have left not one stone on a stone,

But they would have the rabbit out of hiding,

To please the yelping dogs. The gaps I mean,

No one has seen them made or heard them made,

But at spring mending-time we find them there.

I let my neighbor know beyond the hill;

And on a day we meet to walk the line

And set the wall between us once again.

We keep the wall between us as we go.

To each the boulders that have fallen to each.

And some are loaves and some so nearly balls

We have to use a spell to make them balance:

"Stay where you are until our backs are turned!"

We wear our fingers rough with handling them.

Oh, just another kind of out-door game,

One on a side. It comes to little more:

There where it is we do not need the wall:

He is all pine and I am apple orchard.

My apple trees will never get across

And eat the cones under his pines, I tell him.

He only says, "Good fences make good neighbors."

Spring is the mischief in me, and I wonder

If I could put a notion in his head:

"Why do they make good neighbors? Isn't it

Where there are cows? But here there are no cows.

Before I built a wall I'd ask to know

What I was walling in or walling out,

And to whom I was like to give offense.

Something there is that doesn't love a wall,

That wants it down." I could say "Elves" to him,

But it's not elves exactly, and I'd rather

He said it for himself. I see him there

Bringing a stone grasped firmly by the top

In each hand, like an old-stone savage armed.

He moves in darkness as it seems to me,

Not of woods only and the shade of trees.

He will not go behind his father's saying,

And he likes having thought of it so well

He says again, "Good fences make good neighbors."

prepaze

1. When do the neighbors and the author mend their walls?

a) after the hunters damage the wall

b) during spring

c) during dispute

2. Which of these words describes the character trait of the neighbor?

a) considerate

b) philanthropist

c) traditionalist

3. Where does the neighbor reside?

a) in the apple orchard

b) with the hunters

c) beyond the hill

4. How can the author's view be interpreted in these lines?

One on a side. It comes to little more:

There where it is we do not need the wall:

He is all pine and I am apple orchard.

My apple trees will never get across

And eat the cones under his pines.

a) He does not find the wall strong enough to ward off his neighbors.

b) He sees no reason for the wall to be kept.

c) He provides evidence to prove that good fences make good neighbors.

5. What does the reference to fences in this poem symbolize?

a) problem between people

b) relationship between people

c) gap between people

6. Which of these poetic devices is used by the author in this poem?

a) blank verse

b) free verse

c) rhyme scheme

7. Which point of view is used in the poem?

a) first person

b) second person

c) third person

8. Does the author break tradition? Why?

a) Yes. He breaks the tradition by refusing to mend the walls in the end, and he persuades his neighbor to consider his point of view.

b) No. Though the author shows curiosity and questions tradition, he complies to tradition by mending the wall every year just as his neighbor.

c) No. The author is committed to wall building and he explicitly questions the neighbor's choice to keep the wall.

9. Which of these lines is an example for the poetic device "refrain"?

a) But at spring mending-time we find them there.

b) If I could put a notion in his head:

c) Good fences make good neighbours

10. What is the theme of this poem?

a) courage versus perseverance

b) power and corruption

c) openness versus repression

Poem Analysis

1. What are the two contradictory views in this poem?

_____

_____

2. Write the lines expressing a simile and explain the comparison made.

_____

_____

_____

_____

3. What is the significance of the title "Mending Wall"?

_____

_____

_____

_____

Crossword Puzzle

Find the antonyms of the given words in the poem and complete the puzzle.

Across

2. closure

3. obedience

6. damage

7. laugh

Down

1. civilized

4. prey

5. thawed

A Fable

By Mark Twain

Once upon a time an artist who had painted a small and very beautiful picture placed it so that he could see it in the mirror. He said, "This doubles the distance and softens it, and it is twice as lovely as it was before."

The animals out in the woods heard of this through the housecat, who was greatly admired by them because he was so learned, and so refined and civilized, and so polite and high-bred, and could tell them so much which they didn't know before, and were not certain about afterward. They were much excited about this new piece of gossip, and they asked questions, so as to get a full understanding of it. They asked what a picture was, and the cat explained.

"It is a flat thing," he said; "wonderfully flat, marvelously flat, enchantingly flat and elegant. And, oh, so beautiful!"

That excited them almost to a frenzy, and they said they would give the world to see it. Then the bear asked:

"What is it that makes it so beautiful?" "It is the looks of it," said the cat.

This filled them with admiration and uncertainty, and they were more excited than ever. Then the cow asked:

"What is a mirror?"

"It is a hole in the wall," said the cat. "You look in it, and there you see the picture, and it is so dainty and charming and ethereal and inspiring in its unimaginable beauty that your head turns round and round, and you almost swoon with ecstasy."

The ass had not said anything as yet; he now began to throw doubts. He said there had never been anything as beautiful as this before, and probably wasn't now. He said that when it took a whole basketful of sesquipedalian adjectives to whoop up a thing of beauty, it was time for suspicion.

It was easy to see that these doubts were having an effect upon the animals, so the cat went off offended. The subject was dropped for a couple of days, but in the meantime curiosity was taking a fresh start, and there was a revival of interest perceptible. Then the animals assailed the ass for spoiling what could possibly have been a pleasure to them, on a mere suspicion that the picture was not beautiful, without any evidence that such was the case. The ass was not troubled; he was calm, and said there was one way to find out who was in the right, himself or the cat: he would go and look in that hole, and come back and tell what he found there. The animals felt relieved and grateful, and asked him to go at once—which he did.

But he did not know where he ought to stand; and so, through error, he stood between the picture and the mirror. The result was that the picture had no chance, and didn't show up. He returned home and said:

"The cat lied. There was nothing in that hole but an ass. There wasn't a sign of a flat thing visible. It was a handsome ass, and friendly, but just an ass, and nothing more."

The elephant asked:

"Did you see it good and clear? Were you close to it?"

"I saw it good and clear, O Hathi, King of Beasts. I was so close that I touched noses with it."

"This is very strange," said the elephant; "the cat was always truthful before—as far as we could make out. Let another witness try. Go, Baloo, look in the hole, and come and report."

So the bear went. When he came back, he said:

"Both the cat and the ass have lied; there was nothing in the hole but a bear."

Great was the surprise and puzzlement of the animals. Each was now anxious to make the test himself and get at the straight truth. The elephant sent them one at a time.

First, the cow. She found nothing in the hole but a cow. The tiger found nothing in it but a tiger.

The lion found nothing in it but a lion.

The leopard found nothing in it but a leopard. The camel found a camel, and nothing more.

Then Hathi was wroth, and said he would have the truth, if he had to go and fetch it himself. When he returned, he abused his whole subjectry for liars, and was in an unappeasable fury with the moral and mental blindness of the cat. He said that anybody but a near-sighted fool could see that there was nothing in the hole but an elephant.

Moral

You can find in a text whatever you bring, if you will stand between it and the mirror of your imagination. You may not see your ears, but they will be there.

Story Analysis

1. Who informed the animals in the woods about the beautiful picture?

a) artist

b) housecat

c) elephant

2. Which of these words can be used to describe the character trait of the ass?

a) gullible

b) optimist

c) skeptic

3. Who among the animals in the woods first saw the picture?

a) elephant

b) cow

c) ass

4. How did the animals fail to see the picture?

a) by standing in front of the picture and the mirror

b) by standing between the picture and the mirror

c) by standing behind the picture and the mirror

5. What would have happened if the ass had accepted whatever the cat said and admired the picture without evidence?

a) The animals would have raced to see the picture.

b) The animals would have been ignorant of the truth.

c) The animals would have spread the news to others.

6. Which of these statements from the passage is true?

a) It is a flat thing.

b) Both the cat and the ass have lied.

c) Both the statements.

7. What point of view has the author used in this story?

a) first person

b) second person

c) third person

8. What is the theme of the story?

a) knowledge and perspective

b) good versus evil

c) courage and perseverance

9. What can be concluded from this passage?

a) The housecat was smarter than the other animals in the story.

b) The elephant was full of wisdom as it found a way to verify the truth.

c) The ass is the smartest of them all as it is not easily deceived.

10. Which of these statements is parallel to the theme of the story?

a) Humans should stay united in times as crisis as the animals were in the story.

b) Consumers should share a similar perspective to ensure quality products.

c) People often believe any news they hear without analyzing the facts.

Character Analysis

Match the animals from the story with their respective character traits.

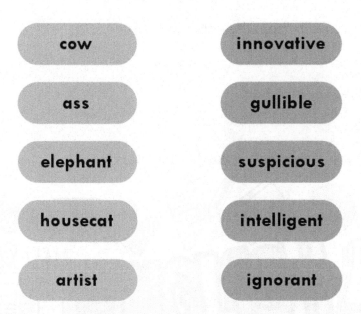

cow

ass

elephant

housecat

artist

innovative

gullible

suspicious

intelligent

ignorant

Sequencing

Arrange the following in the order in which each saw the picture according to the story.

◯ LION

◯ HOUSECAT

◯ LEOPARD

◯ BEAR

◯ TIGER

◯ COW

◯ CAMEL

◯ ELEPHANT

Word Building

Unscramble the words from the passage, and write a paragraph in the box below using at least 5 of these words.

T	E	E	E	H	R	A	L			
L	P	S	S	D	A	E	U	I	E	I	N	Q	A
S	P	C	O	N	U	S	I	I
R	E	I	A	L	V	V
S	I	L	A	S	E	A	D
P	B	L	P	E	R	C	E	E	T	I
D	I	N	E	E	E	V	C
W	N	S	E	S	T	I
R	T	W	H	O
P	P	N	U	A	A	A	E	S	E	B	L

Write your paragraph here. Feel free to use a reference material or the story to learn the usage of the words.

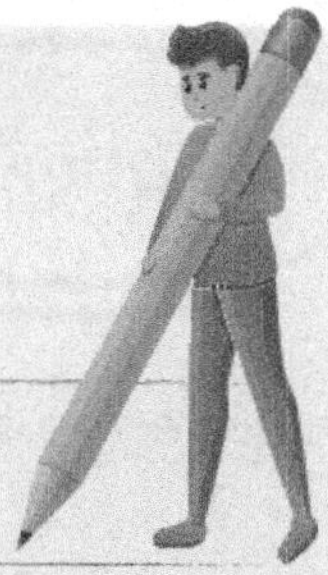

_____

_____

_____

_____

_____

_____

_____

_____

_____

_____

_____

_____

_____

_____

Did You Know?

pneumonoultramicroscopicsilicovolcanoconiosis

This is one of the longest words in the English language.
Find out what it means.

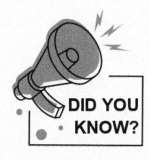

DID YOU
KNOW?

Reading: Informational Text

Beautiful Harbor of Sitka

Read an excerpt from Oregon, Washington and Alaska; Sights and Scenes for the Tourist by E.L. Lomax.

The steamer's whistle is the signal for a holiday in all Alaska ports, and Sitka is no exception to the rule. Six o'clock in the morning, but the sleepy town had awakened to the fact of our arrival, and the inhabitants were out in force to greet friends or sell their canoes.

There are some 1,500 people living in Sitka, including all races. The harbor is the most beautiful a fertile brain can imagine. Exquisitely moulded islands are scattered about in the most enchanting way, all shapes and sizes, with now and then a little garden patch, and ever verdant with native woods and grasses and charming rockeries. As far out as the eye can reach, the beautiful isles break the cold sea into bewitching inlets and lure the mariner to shelter from evil outside waves.

The village nestles between giant mountains on a lowland curve surrounded by verdure too dense to be penetrated with the eye, and too far to try to walk—which is a good excuse for tired feet. The first prominent feature to meet the eye on land is a large square house, two stories high, located on a rocky eminence near the shore, and overlooking the entire town and harbor. Once it was a model dwelling of much pretension, with its spacious apartments, hard-wood six-inch plank floors, elaborately-carved decorations, stained-glass windows, and its amusement and refreshment halls. All betoken the former elegance of the Russian governor's home, which was supported with such pride and magnificence as will never be seen there again. The walls are crumbling, the windows broken, and the old oaken stairways will soon be sinking to earth again, and its only life will be on the page of history.

The mission-school hospital, chapel, and architectural buildings occupied much of the tourists' time, and some were deeply interested.

Understanding Text

1. What does the steamer's whistle signal?

a) rules

b) holiday

c) arrival

2. Why were the inhabitants of the town out by 6 o'clock?

a) to welcome friends

b) to sell canoes

c) both of the above

3. Which of these statements are true according to the author?

a) People of different races live in Sitka.

b) The islands are of different shapes, but similar lengths.

c) The harbor is one of the beautiful places the author has visited.

4. Who do the inlets help according to the author?

a) the steamers

b) the people of the town

c) the mariner

5. What surrounds the town of Sitka that acts as a shield?

a) mountains

b) lush vegetation

c) giant rocks

6. Who was the resident of the large square house by the shore?

a) the mariner

b) the visitors and inhabitants

c) Russian governor

7. What can be inferred from this statement in the third paragraph?

Its only life will be on the page of history.

a) The governor's house was an architectural wonder.

b) The governor's house is no longer feasible for accommodation.

c) The governor's house needs renovation to stay in the pages of history.

8. What attracts the attention of the tourists according to the passage?

a) exquisitely moulded islands

b) architectural buildings

c) Russian governor's home

9. What is the point of view used in this passage?

a) first person

b) second person

c) third person

10. What is the author's purpose in writing this passage?

a) to narrate an experience

b) to persuade tourists

c) to describe the town

Word Building

Use a reference material to understand the following words. Write a new sentence using these words.

1. INHABITANTS

2. EXQUISITE

3. VERDANT

4. ROCKERIES

5. PRETENSION

prepaze

Identify the sentence structure of these sentences from the passage.

1. The steamer's whistle is the signal for a holiday in all Alaska ports, and Sitka is no exception to the rule.

○ simple sentence

○ compound sentence

○ complex sentence

○ compound-complex sentence

2. There are some 1,500 people living in Sitka, including all races.

○ simple sentence

○ compound sentence

○ complex sentence

○ compound-complex sentence

3. Exquisitely moulded islands are scattered about in the most enchanting way, all shapes and sizes, with now and then a little garden patch, and ever verdant with native woods and grasses and charming rockeries.

○ simple sentence

○ compound sentence

○ complex sentence

○ compound-complex sentence

4. As far out as the eye can reach, the beautiful isles break the cold sea into bewitching inlets and lure the mariner to shelter from evil outside waves.

○ simple sentence

○ compound sentence

○ complex sentence

○ compound-complex sentence

5. The walls are crumbling, the windows broken, and the old oaken stairways will soon be sinking to earth again, and its only life will be on the page of history.

○ simple sentence

○ compound sentence

○ complex sentence

○ compound-complex sentence

The graph compares the population rate of 10 countries between the years 2010 and 2020.

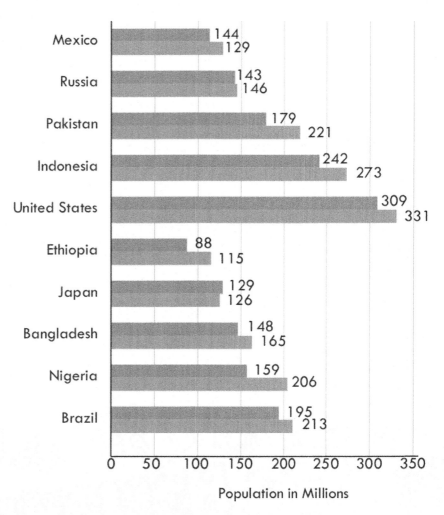

Population in Millions

Source: worldpopulationreview.com, 2020

Study the population trend of the countries given here and answer the questions.

1. What was the population of Indonesia in 2020?

a) 221 million

b) 242 million

c) 273 million

d) 309 million

2. Which country had the population of 148 million in 2010?

a) Bangladesh

b) Russia

c) Japan

d) United States

3. Which country had the lowest population in 2010?

a) Japan

b) Ethiopia

c) Russia

d) Mexico

4. Which country had the highest population in 2020?

a) Indonesia

b) Nigeria

c) Pakistan

d) United States

5. Among the four countries given here, which country is the most populated?

a) Pakistan

b) Russia

c) Ethiopia

d) Bangladesh

6. Which country shows the highest population growth between 2010 and 2020?

a) Indonesia

b) Nigeria

c) Pakistan

d) Brazil

7. Which country shows the lowest population growth between 2010 and 2020?

a) Mexico

b) Nigeria

c) United States

d) Russia

8. Between which two countries is the difference in population vast?

a) Japan - Indonesia

b) United States - Japan

c) Ethiopia - United States

d) Indonesia - Ethiopia

9. According to 2010 data, which of these choices is arranged in ascending order?

a) Pakistan - Russia - Mexico

b) Bangladesh - Nigeria - Japan

c) Mexico - Brazil - Indonesia

d) United States - Pakistan - Indonesia

10. Among the 10 countries, which country shows an opposite trend in population growth?

a) Indonesia

b) Japan

c) Ethiopia

d) United States

Match the country with their flags. Feel free to use any reference material for help.

1. Nigeria

2. Bangladesh

3. Japan

4. Ethiopia

5. United States

6. Pakistan

7. Russia

8. Mexico

9. Brazil

10. Indonesia

Word Building

What are the nationalities of these countries? Find them out using a reference material and complete the table.

Country	Nationality
Nigeria	Nigerian
Bangladesh	
Japan	
Ethiopia	
United States	
Pakistan	
Russia	
Mexico	
Brazil	
Indonesia	

Did You Know?

Did you know that English used to have grammatical gender?

Similar to other languages such as Spanish or French, English used to have grammatical gender.

Aren't we glad English lost its grammatical gender system over time?

Writing

How often do we compete with others for grades or trophies or fame? Are these competitions healthy? Do we need competition in life?

Here are a few popular opinions on this topic.

Competition aides in making successful careers in sports and other fields.

Competition is a double-edged sword.

Judging oneself with respect to others is imperative to set goals.

Learning to lose is not important while growing up.

Competition motivates people to do their best.

Write a 5-paragraph argumentative essay taking a clear stand. Use the below pointers to write the essay.

- Choose a side and stick to it.

- State your stand in the introduction and add a thesis statement.

- Choose 2 reasons to support your stand in two paragraphs and back them with examples.

- In the third body paragraph, acknowledge the opposing view and refute logically with examples.

- Conclude the essay restating your stand clearly and summarizing the reasons.

- Keep the tone and language formal (avoid contractions, informal abbreviations, or slang).

- Third person point of view is preferable to sound unbiased.

Prewriting

First Draft

Editing and Revision Checklist

Use the below checklist to review the first draft, and rewrite the final draft below.

- [ ] Do the first line and introduction get the reader's attention?
- [ ] Do the ideas flow smoothly?
- [ ] Have I acknowledged the opposing views?
- [ ] Is the essay convincing?
- [ ] Am I consistent with the point of view?
- [ ] Am I consistent with the tense throughout?
- [ ] Are the punctuation and capitalization correct?
- [ ] Do the subject and verb agree in each sentence?
- [ ] Have I used complete sentences?
- [ ] Have I used sentences of varied structure?
- [ ] Have I used formal language throughout?

prepaze

Informative Writing

Time to do some research. Do you know how global warming is affecting the temperature? Use any online or print resource to analyze the temperate changes in any 5 countries of your choice.

- Select 5 countries and list them in the table.

- Find the average annual temperature in each country for the past two years and list them accordingly.

- List the data in Fahrenheit. If any source uses Celsius, please convert for consistency.

- Remember to cite the source for reference.

Country	2018 (°F)	2019(°F)

Once the table is complete, draw a graph to represent the data in the above table.

Result of the Study

Write your conclusions and thoughts from the study in a paragraph.

Did any incidental learning happen during this research? If yes, add that as well.

prepaze

Write a narrative in the form of a play. A play includes a narration with dialogs.

Here's an excerpt from *Othello* by William Shakespeare.

ACT I

SCENE I, Venice A. street.

Entter RODERIGO and IAGO

RODERIGO

Tush! never tell me; I take it much unkindly
That thou, Iago, who halt had my purse
As if the strings were thine, shouldst know of this.

IAGO

'Sblood, but you will not hear me:
If ever I did dream of such a matter, Abhor me.

RODERIGO

Thou told'st me thou didst hold him in thy hate.

IAGO

Despise me, if I do not. Three great ones of the city,
In personal suit to make me his lieutenant,
Off-capp'd to him: and, by the faith of man,
I know my price, I am worth no worse a place:
But he; as loving his own pride and purposes,
Evades them, with a bombast circumstance
Horribly stuff'd with epithets of war;
And, in conclusion,
Nonsuits my mediators; for, "Certes," says he,
"I have already chose my officer."

- Notice how the setting "Venice, street" and the characters "Roderigo" and Iago" are introduced.

- Your one-act play should clearly establish the characters and setting.

- Divide the play into scenes.

- Informal language and tone are allowed in narratives.

prepaze

Prewriting

Brainstorm for theme, characters, setting, and plotline.

_____

_____

_____

_____

_____

_____

_____

_____

_____

_____

_____

_____

_____

First Draft

Write your one-act play here.

_____

_____

_____

_____

_____

_____

_____

_____

_____

_____

_____

_____

_____

Editing and Revision Checklist

Use the below checklist to review the first draft, and rewrite the final draft below.

- ☐ Have I given an intriguing title?

- ☐ Have I established the setting (time and place)?

- ☐ Have I established relationships between characters and built character traits through description and action?

- ☐ Have I added commentary in places where necessary?

- ☐ Are the dialogs punctuated correctly?

- ☐ Are the capitalization, pronoun usage, and spelling correct?

- ☐ Do the subject and verb agree in each sentence?

- ☐ Have I used sentences of varied structure?

 **Did You Know?**

William Shakespeare added more than 1000 words to the English Language.

Final Draft

Explanatory Writing

Have you read a book and seen a movie / live production adaptation of the same? Or, have you seen a biopic?

There are many movies and animated films based on books and real events. Oftentimes, the movie makers change the characters or plot to engage the audience.

Think of a book, biopic, or movie and research for your essay. Here are a few popular movie adaptations.

Fictional Books	
Harry Potter	By J. K. Rowling
The Chronicles of Narnia	By C.S.Lewis

Nonfiction/History	
The King's Speech	Inspired by King George VI
The Greatest Showman	A biopic of P. T. Barnum

Prewriting

Compare the movie with the book/history in terms of subtlety, exaggeration, addition of characters or events, plotline, and setting (time and place).

Gather the key details and use the below space for organizing your ideas.

_____

_____

_____

_____

_____

_____

_____

_____

_____

_____

_____

_____

First Draft

Write a comparison essay of 5 paragraphs. The tone can be formal or informal.

Introduction: Introduce the movie and its inspiration. Clearly state in a thesis statement the points you will be comparing in the body paragraphs.

Body paragraphs: Dedicate each paragraph to discuss each point with evidence. Use a point-by-point pattern to compare how each point is dealt in both the media.

Conclusion: Summarize the essay, and evaluate the evidence and points.

Editing and Revision Checklist

Use the below checklist to review the first draft, and rewrite the final draft below.

- ☐ Does the essay have an interesting title?
- ☐ Is the thesis statement placed at the end of the introduction?
- ☐ Does each body paragraph discuss one main idea with examples?
- ☐ Are the evidences reasonable?
- ☐ Can any word be replaced with a better synonym?
- ☐ Is any sentence wordy, vague, or interrupts the flow of ideas?
- ☐ Is the draft consistent in terms of tense and point of view?
- ☐ Are the capitalization, punctuation, and spelling correct?
- ☐ Do the subject and verb agree in each sentence?
- ☐ Have I used sentences of varied structure?

Final Draft

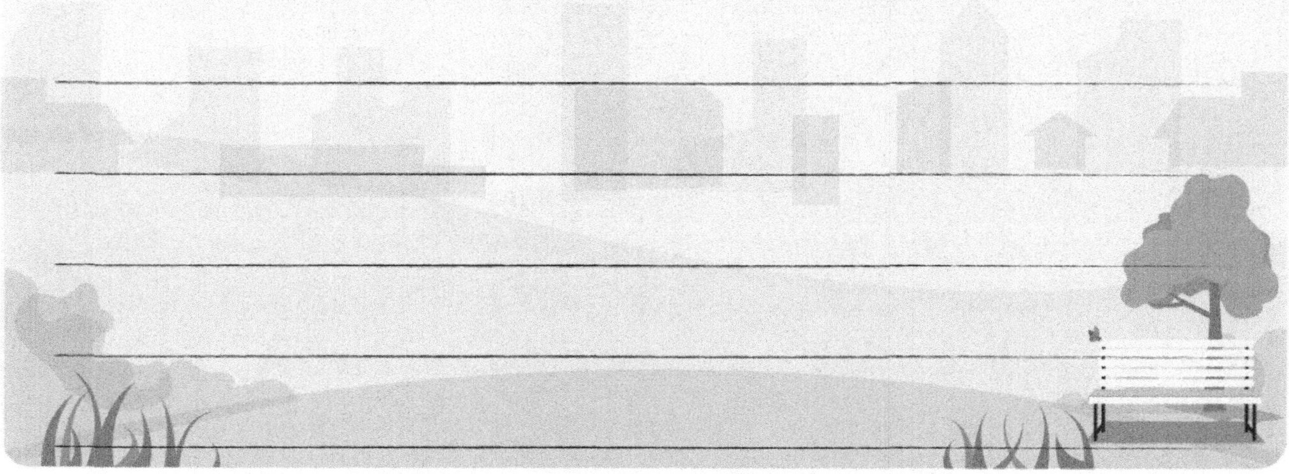

_____

_____

_____

_____

_____

_____

_____

_____

_____

_____

_____

_____

_____

_____

_____

prepaze

94

Math

Use this book to enable your children to explore numbers by solving interesting puzzles and real-life problems. Engage your children with fun, colorful activities and let them fall in love with Math.

Ratio and Proportional Relationship

A proportional relationship is described by the set of ordered pairs that satisfy the equation $y = k\,x$, where k is a positive constant, then k is called the constant of proportionality. For example, if the ratio of y to x is 2 to 3, then the constant of proportionality is $\frac{2}{3}$, and $y = \frac{2}{3}\,x$.

A proportional relationship is a correspondence between two types of quantities such that the measures of quantities of the first type are proportional to the measures of quantities of the second type.

Let's practice

Ratio

Express each count as ratio and fraction.

a. gray flowers to black flowers

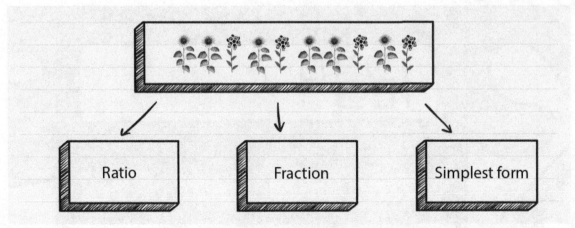

Ratio	Fraction	Simplest form

b. cactus to grass

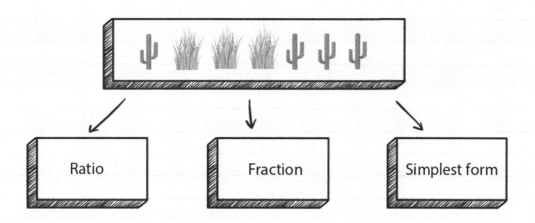

| Ratio | Fraction | Simplest form |

c. palm tree to apple tree

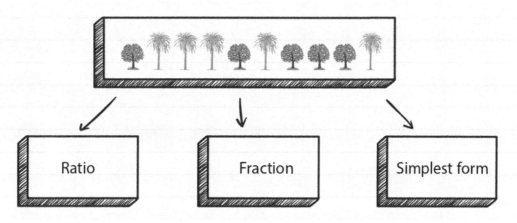

| Ratio | Fraction | Simplest form |

Percentage Representation

Color the figure with the correct percentage representation.

a.

2 days out of 5 working days

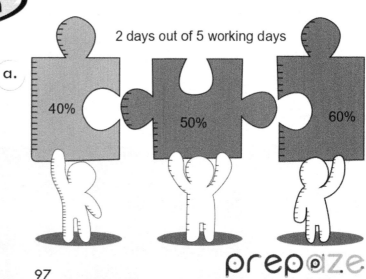

40%

50%

60%

prepaze

b.

3 baseballs to 8 footballs

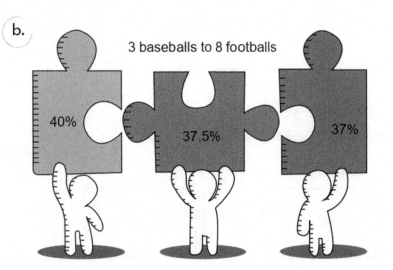

40%

37.5%

37%

c.

5 cookies to 4 cupcakes

120%

125%

25%

Unit Rate

Find the unit rate.

a. There are 280 kids and 5 teachers. What is the number of kids to be managed by each teacher?

b. There are 40 chocolates in a box. If each child gets $\frac{1}{8}$th of the total chocolates, how many children are there?

c. Alex walks $\frac{1}{3}$ of a mile in 18 minutes. What is his unit rate in miles per hour?

Help Fedrick decide on the best deal.

a.

A pack of 6 oranges @ $4

A pack of 4 oranges @ $3

b.

A pack of 4 eggs @ $3

A pack of 3 eggs @ $1.50

c.

2 gallons of milk

@ $1.80

1.5 gallon of milk

@ $3

d.

A pack of 10 pens

@ $6

A pack of 6 pens

@ $6

a. Oranges :

b. Eggs :

c. Milk :

d. Pens :

25% of the class of 40 kids are girls. Express the ratio of girls to boys as a simple fraction. If girls and boys form teams consisting of 4 members how many boys and how many girls constitute each team and total how many teams can be formed. (Hint: Find the unit rate).

Sam works in a garage and he works 8 hours a day. On Monday, he completed maintenance of 30% of the vehicles of the 20 given for service in 6 hours. How many more would be complete at the end of day. (Hint: Find the unit rate)

In a written examination, Rob attempts 400 questions and gets 240 correct answers and Sam attempts 520 questions and gets 320 correct. The total number of questions in the test is 600 questions.

a. What is the ratio of the number of questions Rob attempted to the total number of questions?	
b. What is the ratio of correct answers of Rob to correct answers of Sam?	
c. What is the ratio of percentage of correct answers attempted by Rob to the percentage of correct answers attempted by Sam?	

Proportional Relationships

Which Variety Would Cost Less?

Look at the price list at Frank's fruit stall. Which variety of apples cost least per pound? Draw an apple in the correct row.

Apple Variety	Price per packet	Draw here
Fuji	$4.8 / 2 lbs	
Washington red	$3.90 / 3 lbs	
Honeydew	$5.70 / 3 lbs	
Green	$5.20 / 4 lbs	

Rita wants to sketch a building design. She decided to scale 1 inch for each foot of the building. If the building planned is 20 feet * 50 feet, what is the measure of the rectangle sketched by Rita?

State true or false?

a. The ratio $\dfrac{7}{14}$ and $\dfrac{1}{2}$ is proportional _____

b. The ratio $\dfrac{5}{6}$ and $\dfrac{2}{3}$ is proportional _____

c. The ratio $\dfrac{2}{6}$ and $\dfrac{3}{9}$ is proportional _____

d. The ratio of 3 oranges and 7 apples to 5 oranges and 3 apples is proportional _____

e. The ratio of \$40 for 2 hours to \$60 for 5 hours is proportional _____

Solve the proportion.

a. $\dfrac{3}{x} = \dfrac{5}{4}$	b. $\dfrac{12}{e} = \dfrac{60}{7}$
c. $\dfrac{10}{3} = \dfrac{5}{x}$	d. $\dfrac{18}{4} = \dfrac{y}{6}$

Equation of Proportionality

Derive equation of proportionality from graph.

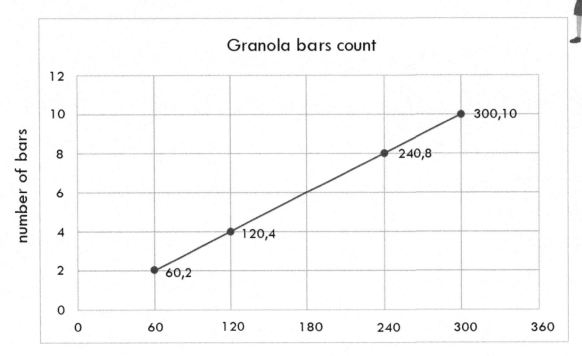

Granola bars count

60,2
120,4
240,8
300,10

number of bars

weight in grams

a. Find unit rate.

b. Derive the equation of the line graph.

c. Explain slope and intercept in terms of parameters explained in the graph.

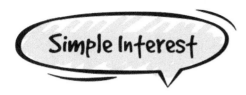

Simple Interest

If Gary borrows $5000 for 4% simple interest to be paid at the end of every year for 5 years.

a. Complete the table.

Period (x)	Accumulated interest (y)
1	
2	
3	
4	
5	

b. What is the unit rate?

c. Graph the data and find the equation explaining the relationship.

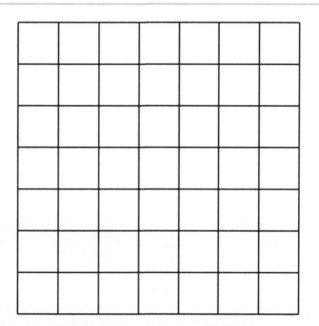

d. Explain the relationship of x to y.

The Tax Problem

The sales tax for various receipt amounts is as below.

Purchase amount $	Tax per receipt
42.5	3.55
60	4.6
72.5	5.35
100	7

a. What is the unit rate?

_____

b. Graph the data and find the equation explaining the relationship.

prepaze

c. Explain the relationship of x to y.

_____

In an experiment to study the effect of immunization, 400 mice were inoculated with pathogens. After immunization, 280 mice were unaffected and rest developed symptoms.

a. What is the ratio of immune to diseased?

b. What is the percentage vulnerable to the total population?

The Number System

A negative number is a number less than zero.

Adding an integer to a number can be represented on a number line as counting up when the integer is positive (just like whole numbers) and counting down when the integer is negative.

Subtracting a number is the same as adding its opposite. For example: $(5 - 4) + 4 = 5$.

The absolute value of a number is the distance between the number and zero on the number line.

A rational number is a number that can be represented as a fraction or the opposite of a fraction.

Using a formula, the distance between rational numbers, p and q, is $|p - q|$

Let's practice

Rational Numbers

Represent the shaded portions in gray in the form of $\frac{p}{q}$, where $\frac{p}{q}$ is a rational number.

  a.

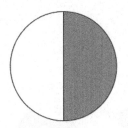

b.

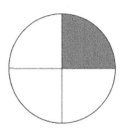

c.

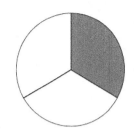

d. Add all the above $\frac{p}{q}$ forms.

Classify the Numbers

Classify numbers as a whole number, integer, rational number.

a. $-4, \frac{1}{2}, 2.3, -\frac{3}{5}$

b. $6, -8, -\frac{3}{5}, 0, \frac{1}{3}$

c. $0.45, -\frac{12}{19}, 32, -56, \sqrt{49}$

Rational	Whole Number	Integer

Write the absolute and opposite values of the following numbers.

Number	Absolute value	Opposite value
a. $-\dfrac{12}{17}$		
b. 1.34		
c. $-\sqrt{4}$		

In the number line locate the following.

a. -5

b. $\dfrac{5}{8}$

c. $\sqrt{3}$

On the number line show the following operations.

a. $-4 + 2 =$

b. $3 + (-2) =$

c. $7 - (-1) =$

On the number line locate the following.

a. $\frac{1}{2} + 3\frac{1}{4}$

b. $-2.3 + 3$

c. $4.8 - 2.3$

Evaluate the following.

a. $(\frac{2}{7} \times 28) - 10 =$

b. $\frac{50}{9} - \frac{24}{11} =$

c. $\frac{2}{4}(12 - \frac{3}{7}) =$

Convert to fractions.

a. $2\frac{3}{5}$

b. $12\frac{5}{7}$

c. 11.35

Convert to decimals.

a. $\frac{245}{8}$

b. $\frac{108}{7}$

c. $21\frac{6}{7}$

prepaze

How Much Does Sam Save?

Sam earns $3000 per month. He pays rent for $2000. The rest of the expenses are shown in the picture below. How much does he save at the end of the month?

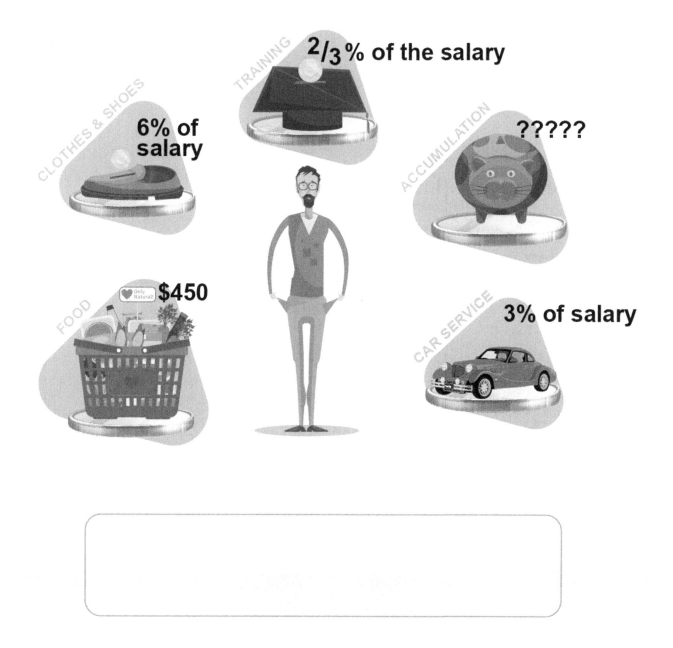

CLOTHES & SHOES — **6% of salary**

TRAINING — **2/3% of the salary**

ACCUMULATION — **?????**

FOOD — **$450**

CAR SERVICE — **3% of salary**

Complete the grid such that the sum of numbers in each row is equal to ½.

	$\dfrac{2}{8}$	$\dfrac{1}{8}$
$\dfrac{1}{12}$		$\dfrac{2}{12}$
$\dfrac{1}{14}$	$\dfrac{2}{14}$	

Gina visits a very strange city where the temperatures change drastically. On Monday the temperature dipped to −14 degrees F but the next day it was sunny and the temperature rose by 40 degrees F. What is the temperature on Tuesday?

April 16
Monday   11:42 PM

AwesomeCity

-14°F

Real Feel: 18°
Wind: N-E, 5-8 km/h
Pressure: 1000 MB   Sunrise: 6.02 AM
Humidity: 51%   Sunset: 9:18 PM

Tuesday

Allen, Lisa, and John were doing their homework. Lisa takes twice the time that Allen takes to complete her homework. John takes $\frac{2}{3}$rd time that Lisa takes to complete. If John completes the homework in 2 hours.

a. How long does Lisa take to complete her homework?

b. Who takes the least time to complete and by how much?

c. Arrange the names of the children according to the time taken in the order of least to highest.

prepaze

An Eggey Problem

At Spicey treats, Rose grinds fresh pepper for a particular egg recipe, every day. For every 1 gm of pepper pods, she gets 0.8 gm of powder.

a. If a 12–gram pepper pod is fried, how much powder does she get?

b. If she uses all of the powder to sprinkle 16 boiled eggs equally, how much powder did she sprinkle on each egg?

Find the unknown.

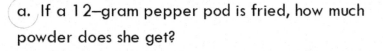

a. $5 \times (\frac{4}{3} + \frac{1}{3}) = 5 \times (x) + 5 \times \frac{1}{3}$

b. $(\frac{6}{7} \times \frac{4}{5}) \times \frac{3}{2} = \frac{6}{7} \times (z \times \frac{3}{2})$

Expressions and Equations

VARIABLE (DESCRIPTION): A variable is a symbol (such as a letter) that represents a number (i.e., it is a placeholder for a number).

NUMERICAL EXPRESSION (DESCRIPTION): A numerical expression is a number, or it is any combination of sums, differences, products, or divisions of numbers that evaluates to a number.

VALUE OF A NUMERICAL EXPRESSION: The value of a numerical expression is the number found by evaluating the expression. An expression is a numerical expression, or it is the result of replacing some (or all) of the numbers in a numerical expression with variables.

Two expressions are equivalent if both expressions evaluate to the same number for every substitution of numbers into all the letters in both expressions.

An expression written as sums (and/or differences) of products whose factors are numbers, variables, or variables raised to whole number powers is said to be in expanded form. A single number, variable, or a single product of numbers and/or variables is also considered to be in expanded form. Examples of expressions in expanded form include: 324, $3x$, $5x + 3$

Each summand of an expression in expanded form is called a term. For example, the expression $2y + 5y + 3$ consists of three terms: $2y$, $5y$, 3

The number found by multiplying just the numbers in a term together is the coefficient of the term. For example, given the product $5 \times y \times 2$, its equivalent term is $10y$. The number 10 is called the coefficient of the term $10y$.

Let's practice

Equivalent Expressions

Write equivalent expressions by combining like terms. One is done for you.

a.

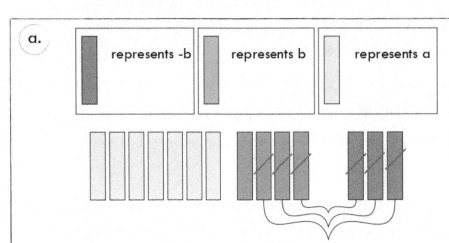

represents -b

represents b

represents a

$7a + 4b - 3b = 7a + b$

b.

represents 1 unit

represents x

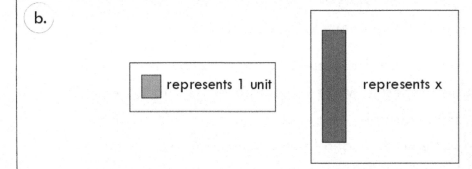

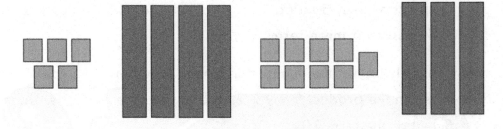

$5 + 4x + 9 + 3x =$

prepaze

c.

represents x

represents y

represents -y

Write the expression as well as the equivalent expression.

$$\boxed{} = \boxed{}$$

d.

represents v

represents -1 unit

Write the expression as well as the equivalent expression.

$$\boxed{} = \boxed{}$$

Expression in Standard form

Write the expression in standard form.

a. $2(2a) + 5(-6b) + (5.c.8)$	=
b. $8.a.2 + 7.(-b).2 + 3(7c)$	=
c. $(-5).a.(6) + 9.b - 2.(9c)$	=

Write equivalent expressions by combining like terms. Verify the equivalence of your expression and the given expression by evaluating the given values in each problem.

a. $4a - a$ for $a = -2$ →

→ b. $6b - 2b + 3b$ for $b = -1$

c. $9c + 2c - 3c$ for $c = 3$ →

→ d. $5x - 8x - 2x$ for $x = 1/5$

e. $-6y - 4y + 20y$ for $y = -1/10$ →

prepaze

Who Is Right?

Explain who is right and who is wrong with an appropriate reason.

Reason:

Reason:

Anna:
I wrote the equivalent expression as 2 + 15y.
Am I right?

Samuel:
I wrote the equivalent expression as 15 + 2y.
Am I right?

$6y + 9y + 2$

Solve the following.

a. Find the result when $-12m + 6$ is added to $3m - 11$

b. Find the result when 9g is subtracted from 5g − 8.

c. What is the result when −5x +2 is taken away from −8x −9?

Represent as Expressions

Write the equivalent expressions.

a. A guitar is on sale for 15% off from the original price. Let "m" represent the original price. Write two expressions that can be used to calculate the sale price.

SPECIAL OFFER
SHOP NOW!

Expression 1	Expression 2

b. There are "n" motorists in a motorcycle race. ¾ of the motorists finish the race. How many did not finish the race?

c. Cost of a football is "d" dollars. The sales tax is 6%. Write two expressions that can be used to calculate the total cost of the football, including tax.

Expression 1	Expression 2

d. Julia had a long piece of ribbon. She cuts it into "y" pieces, each 10 cm long and one piece of 5 cm long. What is the total length of the ribbon?

e. Paul goes for dinner. He leaves a tip of 12% on the bill. What expressions can be used to represent the total cost of his dinner, including tax?

Expression 1	Expression 2

Simplify the expression.

a. 2g – 3 (1 + 5g)

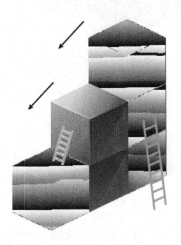

b. (h + 9) + 2 (h + 8)

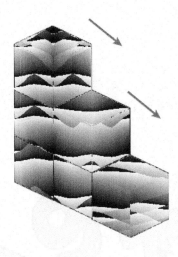

c. $5j + 2(j + 2k) + 3k$

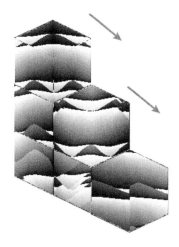

d. $3(2 + 7a) + 5a$

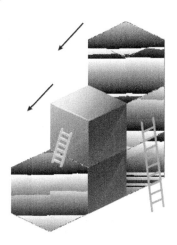

e. $8m + 2n - 7(2m - 5n)$

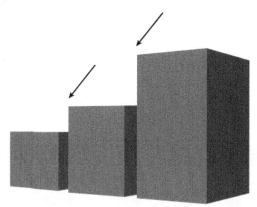

prepaze

Write the expressions for the perimeter of the given 2D shapes.

a.
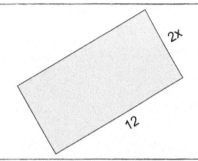

b.
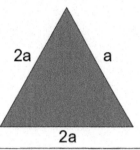

c.

d.
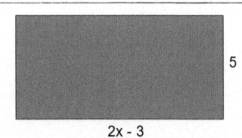

e.
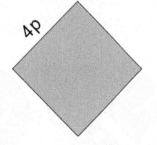

Solve the Problems

Solve the following problems.

a. A park is in the shape of a quadrilateral with the sides of ratio 1:2:3:4. Write the expression to find the perimeter of the park.

b. Richard's garden is in the shape of a rectangle. The sides have a ratio 5:4:5:4. Write an expression to find the perimeter of the backyard garden?

c. There are "x" people on a bus. At Waterfront station, 12 people boarded the bus while 5 alighted. How many people are on a bus now?

Olivia goes to the zoo with her family. Each member buys a ticket and five packets of bird feed. There are five members in her family. Let "m" represent the cost of a ticket and "n" represent the cost of a packet of bird feed. Write two different expressions that represent the total amount her family spent. Explain how each expression describes the situation in a different way.

Array Problem

Use the following rectangular array to answer the questions below.

a. Fill in the missing information.

?	?	?
16	8n	4m

(with **?** on the left side as well)

b. Write the sum represented in the rectangular array.

c. Justify the area of the above rectangle using "length x breadth" and see if it is the same as the sum represented in part b.

Rewrite the expression in standard form. Justify each step.

a. Find the sum of $9x + 15$ and the opposite of 15.

b. Find the sum of the multiplicative inverse of 7 and $-9y$.

c. Find the product of $8m + 40$ and the multiplicative inverse of 8.

d. Find the product of $-9a + 45$ and the multiplicative inverse of -9

e. Subtract the opposite of $7x$ from $-10x + 9$

Write the indicated expressions.

a. The perimeter of an equilateral triangle with $\dfrac{4}{5}$ k cm sides.

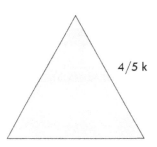

b.

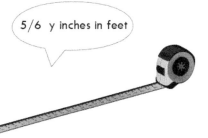

5/6 y inches in feet

c. The number of pounds in 6x oz.

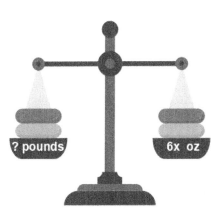

? pounds   6x oz

d. 5x grams in kilogram

e. The average speed of a car that travels x miles in $\dfrac{1}{2}$ hour. (hint: speed = distance/time)

Distributive Property

Rewrite the expressions by using the distributive property and collecting like terms.

a.

$$\frac{7}{8} \ (16y - 8)$$

b.

$$\frac{5}{7} \ (\frac{7}{9}a - \frac{1}{5})$$

c.

$$2\frac{3}{5}b - \frac{2}{3} \ (2b + \frac{1}{5})$$

d.

$$\frac{1}{6} \ (p + 6) + \frac{7}{8} \ (p - 2)$$

e.

$$\frac{2x + 3}{6} + \frac{x - 4}{12}$$

Find the Errors

Given table shows the problems with incorrect solutions. Find the errors and write the correct solutions.

Problems with incorrect solutions	What is the mistake?	Correct solution with steps
5x + 2(4x) – 7 Step 1: 5x + 8x – 7 Step 2: 6x		
12 – 4 (7 – y) Step 1: 8(7 – y) Step 2: 56 – 8y		
11v – 2(–2v + 5) Step 1: 11v + 4v + 10 Step 2: 15v + 10		

Math Maze

Complete the maze by solving the one step equations. Draw the path to reach the finish.

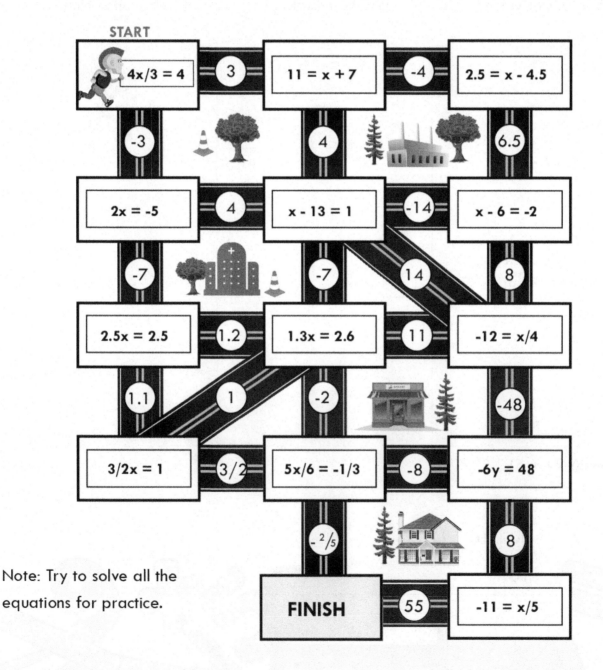

Note: Try to solve all the equations for practice.

prepaze

Match the equations which have the same x value.

$$x/3 - 5 = 3$$

$$2x - 92 = -2x + 36$$

$$x/8 + 11 = 15$$

$$-5x - 5 = -25$$

$$-4 + 4x = 12$$

$$-5x + 12 = -2x - 33$$

$$2x/3 - 7 = 3$$

$$-25 + 2x = 23$$

Check whether the given value of x is a solution to the equation. Justify your answer.

a. $\dfrac{4x}{3} = 5x + 1 \qquad x = 12$

b. $2x + 9 = x + 10 \qquad x = -4\dfrac{1}{3}$

c. $\dfrac{1}{5}(x + 5) = 12 \qquad x = 50$

d. $\dfrac{3}{5} + x = 2x + 3 \qquad x = -1\dfrac{1}{5}$

e. $\dfrac{1}{4}x + 4 = 6 + \dfrac{1}{5}x \qquad x = 40$

Solve the problems.

a. The perimeter of a rectangle is 28 inches. If its length is three times its width, find the dimensions.

b. The sum of two consecutive odd numbers is 72. Find the numbers.

c. Fardin and Jack together have $15.55. Fardin has $5.25 less than Jack. How much money does each person have?

d. Ronaldo is 7 years younger than Jackson. In 5 years, the sum of their ages will be 67 years. How old is Jackson and Ronaldo?

e. Two numbers are in the ratio 6:4. If they differ by 18, find these numbers.

Solve the Inequalities

Solve the inequalities and represent on the number line. One is done for you.

a. $x + 5 > 4$

○ This value is not included in the solution $\qquad$ $x + 5 - 5 > 4 - 5$

● This value is included in the solution $\qquad$ $x > -1$

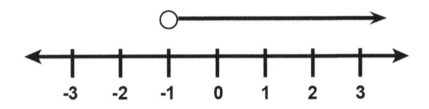

b. $3x - 5 > 2x - 4$

c. $-4x \leq 16$

d. $0 > 6 - 3x$

e. $5x \leq 9 + 2x$

Solve the problems with or without using variables.

a. Benjamin runs a small library. Every month, Benjamin receives a membership fee of $15 from each of the members. Last month, the library had 50 members. This month, 30 new members joined, and 10 members canceled their membership. How much money will Benjamin earn this month?

b. James has $80. He buys a woolen jacket for $32 and 3 scarfs. Each scarf costs the same. Find the cost of one scarf.

c. Mary goes for an exhibition. She had $150. She spent $60 for some wooden antiques. She also purchased a carpet for $48 and 2 chairs. Each of the chairs cost the same. Write an equation representing the cost of all the items and determine the cost of each product.

d. Noah buys some snacks for his sister's birthday party. He had $90. He buys a pineapple cake for $25, a packet of toffees for $15, and 10 birthday caps. Each birthday cap costs the same price. Write an equation representing the total expenditure of the party and determine the price of one cap.

prepaze

Write the inequality which produces the range shown in the number line. One is done for you.

a. ○⟶ -3 -2 -1 0 1 2 3	$x > 1$
b. ○⟶ -4 -3 -2 -1 0 1 2 3 4	
c. ●⟶ -3 -2 -1 0 1 2 3	
d. ⟵○ -4 -3 -2 -1 0 1 2 3 4	
e. ⟵● -4 -3 -2 -1 0 1 2 3 4	

Describe the Banner Length

Sophia's class students are making a banner for their school program. The length of the banner should be 20 ft. The students can use 48 ft or less than that of trim around and outside the banner.

a. Create an inequality describing the restriction of the size of the banner.

b. Graph the solution set.

c. What are the possible widths of the banner?

Mr.Jackson buys a car for \$15,000. The value of the car is $15,000 \left(1 - \dfrac{n}{5}\right)$ after n years. He decided to replace the car when the trade-in value is \$6,000. After how many years should he plan to replace the car in order to receive this trade-in value?

Lucas loves to go on weekend trips. On one such trip he rode 90 miles in 5 hours. He rode at an average speed of 18 mph for t hours and at an average speed of 21 mph for the rest of the time. How long did Lucas ride at the slower speed? Use the variable t to represent the time, in hours, Lucas rode at 18 mph.

	Rate (mph)	Time (hours)	Distance (miles)
Lucas speed 1			
Lucas speed 2			

The total cost of two shirts and one pair of trousers is $59.88. The cost of each shirt is $15.14 .

a. Using an arithmetic approach, find the cost of the pair of trousers.

b. Let the cost of a shirt be **y** dollars. Write an expression for the total cost of two shirts and one pair of trousers in terms of **y**.

c. Write an equation that could be used to find the cost of a shirt.

d. Solve the equation in part c to find the value of **y**.

Write the equation and solve.

a.

I am thinking of a number. If you multiply my number by 6, add 6 to the product, and then take 12 of the sum, the result is 6. Find my number.

b.

The sum of a number, $\frac{1}{2}$ of that number, $2\frac{1}{3}$ of that number, and 12 is $4\frac{1}{3}$. Find the number.

c.

Olivia thinks of a number and subtracts $\frac{1}{2}$ from it. She multiplies the result by 6. The final result is 3 times her original number.

Find the number.

Write an inequality to represent the situation described below and use them to solve for the unknown variable.

Myra is planning for a vacation. The hotel costs $40 per night and her flights cost $140. She has a budget of $500 for hotel and flights. Up to how many nights can she afford in the hotel?

Benjamin ordered 30 t-shirts and 30 coffee mugs for printing. The t-shirts printing cost is 15 cents more than printing coffee mugs. If Benjamin's order costs $139.50, find the printing cost of each t-shirt and coffee mug.

James is confused between which cell phone plans to choose. The first plan charges 24 cents per minute. The second plan charges a monthly fee of $ 32.39 plus 6 cents per minute. How many minutes James would have to use in a month in order for the second plan to be preferable? (Round the answer to the nearest whole number)

Geometry

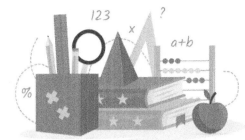

The surface of a pyramid is the union of its base region and its lateral faces. Two triangles satisfy the three sides condition if there is a triangle correspondence between the two triangles such that each pair of corresponding sides are equal in length.

A triangle correspondence between two triangles is a pairing of each vertex of one triangle with one and only one vertex of the other triangle. A triangle correspondence also induces a correspondence between the angles of the triangles and the sides of the triangles.

Two triangles are said to have identical measures if there is a triangle correspondence such that all pairs of corresponding sides are equal in length and all pairs of corresponding angles are equal in measure. Two triangles with identical measures are sometimes said to be identical.

Let's practice

Scale Drawings

Find the scale factor using the scale drawing and the actual drawing.

a. Express your answer as a fraction.

Actual length: 5 in   Scale length: 3 in

b. Use these two drawings to complete the table.

2.45 in

1.5 in

Drawing 1

3.92 in

2.4 in

Drawing 2

	Quotient of corresponding horizontal distances	Quotient of corresponding vertical distances	Scale factor as a percentage
Drawings 2 to 1			

c. The scale factor from brick 1 to 2 is 60%. Find the scale factor from shape 2 to 1. Will this be a reduction or an enlargement?

Brick 1

Brick 2

d. The scale factor from Shape 1 to 2 is 40% and the scale factor from shape 2 to 3 is 37.5%. What is the scale factor from Shape 1 to 3. Explain your reasoning. Show a verification using an example.

1

2

3

e. Find the scale factor of the new scale drawing to the original scale drawing using the given information.

Original scale factor - 20

New scale factor - 25

1 m   1 m

125 cm   125 cm

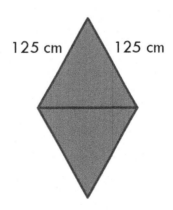

Scale factor -

Draw scale drawings for each of these:

a. A family portrait is 3 feet by 3 feet in dimensions. Use a scale factor $\frac{1}{18}$ to make a scale drawing.

b. Create a scale drawing of this pencil using a scale factor of 150%.

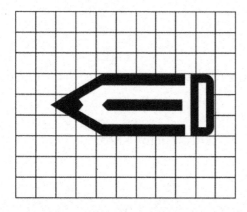

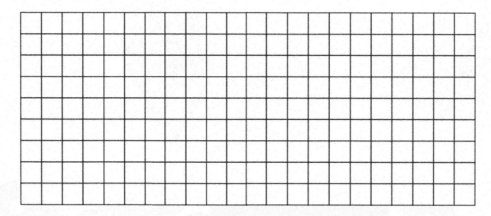

Is the scale drawing an enlargement or a reduction? Explain how you know.

c. Fiona has a small patch of garden which is 12 ft long and 5 ft wide.

12 ft

5 ft

Olivia's garden is 60% the length of Fiona's and 125% wider than Fiona's. Find the dimensions of Olivia's garden. Make a scale drawing where 1ft = 1cm.

Word Problems

Solve these word problems.

a. Mathew made a model of a rocket with 2.5 feet as the length and 1.25 feet as the wing span. If the length of the actual rocket is 184 feet. Find the actual length of the wing span using an equation.

b. An artist plans to paint one of her paintings onto a wall using a projected image. Her reference image is 2 inches long. How long will her mural be if the projector uses a scale to represent 1 inch of the reference image as 2 ½ ft on the wall.

c. Here are 3 images of a postcard.

The dimensions of the smallest postcard is 6 inches by 8 inches and the medium postcard is 10 inches by $13\frac{1}{3}$ inches.

Part A - If the medium postcard is a scale of the smallest postcard, what is the scale factor?

Part B - The large postcard has a scale factor of 250% compared to the smallest postcard. What are the dimensions of this large postcard?

Part C - What percentage of the area of the larger postcard is the area of the medium sized postcards?

Find the Areas

Find the areas:

a. Here are two images of a pizza in a box.

10 in

6 in

The bigger box has 21.5 square inch of free space. Write an equation that relates area and scale factor of big to small and explain what each quantity represents. Determine the area of the free space in the smaller box.

b. A scale drawing of Yulu's Stationary store is given. Find the actual area of the store.

Scale: 1 inch on the drawing corresponds to 15 feet in actual length

2 inch

$1^1/2$ inch

Fill in the table with the names of the angles by referring to the diagram.

79°

53°

48°

A ← ——————— E ——————— → B

53°

90°

37°

C

F

D

G

Vertical angles	
Adjacent angles	
Angles on a line	
Angles at a point	

Angle Measures

Find the angle measures for each of these:

a. Let x represent the measurement of an acute angle in degrees. The ratio of the complement of x to the supplement of x is 2: 5. Guess and check to determine the value of x. Explain why your answer is correct.

b. Two lines and two rays meet at a point. Use appropriate equations to solve for m and n. Describe their angle relationships while using each equation.

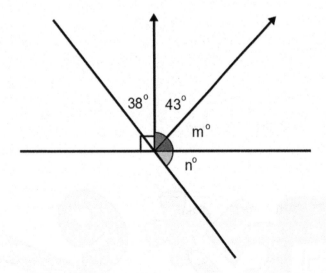

c. Write an equation to find the value of x, then find the angles ∢AOB and ∢BOC.

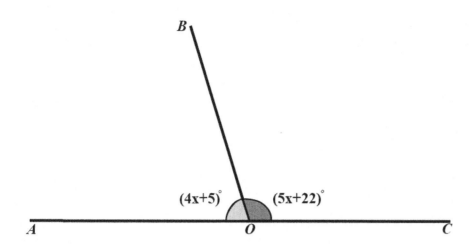

$(4x+5)°$ $(5x+22)°$

d. Three lines and three rays meet at a point. Find the values of x and y using appropriate equations.

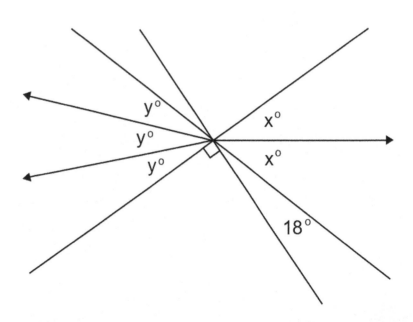

Angle Fun

Draw the following as per the given instructions.

a. Draw supplementary angles so that one angle is 36°. Label each angle with its measurement.

b. Draw a rectangle EFGH with EF= 4 cm and FG = 7 cm. Mark your measurements.

c. The table contains information for a parallelogram PQRS. Make a rough sketch without any tools. Then, use a ruler, protractor, and set square to draw an accurate parallelogram.

Fill in the table with the missing measurements.

∢ P	PQ	Altitude to PQ	QR	Altitude to QR
45°	5 cm		4 cm	

d. Use a set square, ruler, and protractor to draw rhombus WXYZ so that the measurement of ∢ W is 60°, and each side of the rhombus measures 5 cm.

prepaze

e. Draw an isosceles trapezoid ABCD with two equal base angles, $\angle A$ and $\angle B$, such that each measures $110°$. Use your compass to create the two equal sides of the trapezoid. Leave arc marks as evidence of the use of your compass. Label all angle measurements. Explain how you constructed the trapezoid.

f. Use any one condition that makes a triangle unique and draw it. Label your drawing and mention the measurements. Explain the condition that you chose.

Constructing Triangles

Explain each of these scenarios.

a. Derek says that he constructed a triangle with two of its angles measuring 140° and 80°. Show a construction to show he is wrong. Explain your drawing and include labels.

prepaze

b. For each of these pairs of triangles, write if they are identical, non-identical, or not necessarily identical. Justify your answer.

Triangles	Identical/non-identical/ not necessarily identical.	Justification

The Bridge Problem

The bridge below, which crosses a river, is built out of two triangular supports. The point M lies on BC. The beams represented by AM and DM are equal in length, and the beams represented by AB and DC are equal in length. If the supports were constructed so that ∢A and ∢D are equal in measurement, is point M the midpoint of BC? Explain.

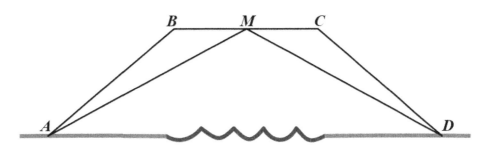

Slice as a 2D Shape

Draw slices at an angle for the right rectangular prism and the right rectangular pyramid given. Draw a 2D shape of your slice.

a. A pentagon		Slice as a 2D shape
b. A hexagon		Slice as a 2D shape
c. A quadrilateral		Slice as a 2D shape
d. A pentagon		Slice as a 2D shape

In the following figure, use a straightedge to join the points where a slicing plane meets with a right rectangular prism to outline the slice.

i. Label the vertices of the rectangular slice WXYZ.

ii. State any known dimensions of the slice.

iii. Describe two relationships the slice WXYZ has in relation to faces of the right rectangular prism

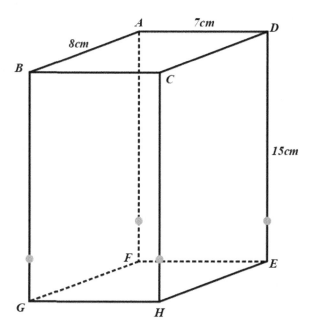

A top view of a right rectangular pyramid is given. The line segments lie in the base face. For each line segment, sketch a slice that results from slicing the right rectangular pyramid with a place that contains the line segment and is perpendicular to the base.

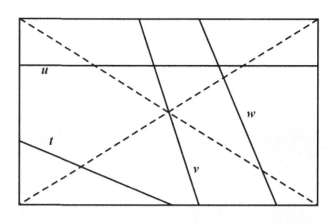

Circle Problems

Find solutions to these word problems.

a. If you know only the diameter of a circle, what other measurements can you find? Explain how you can use the diameter to find all the other measurements.

b. A ceramic potter created a ring using a pottery wheel as shown below. Fred drew a two-dimensional image of the ring. What is the area of this ring given the inner radius of 5 cm and the outer radius of 9 cm?

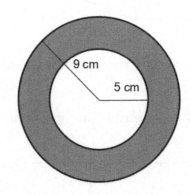

c. Peter is fixing his doorway. He decides to use 2 quarter circles of glass and 2 squares pieces of glass to cover up an arch above his door, as shown below.

If the length of the bottom part of this arrangement is 12 feet. How much glass does Peter need to complete his job?

d. If one circle has a diameter of 10 m and a second circle has a diameter of 20 m, what is the ratio of the area of the larger circle to the area of the smaller circle?

prepaze

The Role of circumference

Solve each of the following.

a. Find the perimeter of the shape. It is made of one semi-circle and one rectangle.

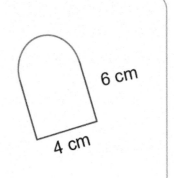

6 cm

4 cm

b. Find the area of the semi-circle.

5 m

c. The area of a circle is 36 π cm^2. Find the circumference.

prepaze

Area, Volume, and Surface Area

Find the area of the shaded portion for each of these given shapes.

a.

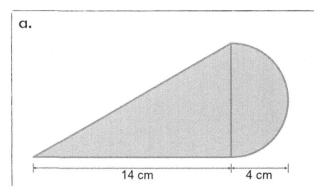

14 cm   4 cm

b. This shape is made of two semi-circles and a quarter of a circle.

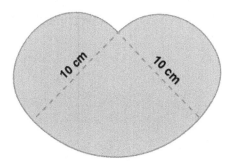

10 cm   10 cm

c.

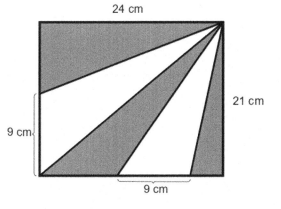

24 cm

21 cm

9 cm

9 cm

d.

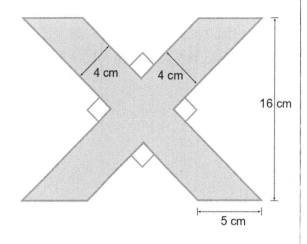

4 cm   4 cm

16 cm

5 cm

prepaze

How Much Water?

An apartment has a rectangular tank to harvest rainwater. The dimensions of the tank are 20 feet long, 8 feet wide, and 6 feet deep.

a. How much water can the tank hold?

b. If there are 7.48 gallons in 1 cubic foot, how many gallons are needed to fill the tank?

c. When the tank was full, about 1198.6 gallons of water leaked from the tank. How many feet did the water level drop?

d. After the leak was repaired, it was necessary to lay a thin layer of concrete to protect the sides of the tank. Calculate the area to be covered to complete the job.

prepaze

Find the surface area of each of these solids.

a.

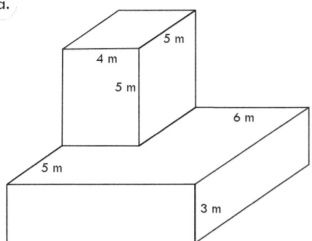

b.

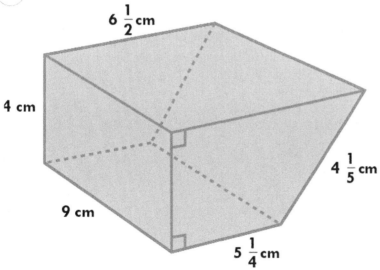

c.

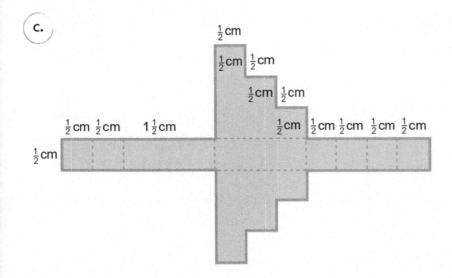

d. In the diagram, there are 14 cubes glued together to form a solid. Each cube has a volume of $\dfrac{1}{8}$ in^3. Find the surface area of the solid.

Calculate the volume of each prism.

a.

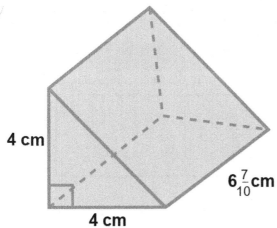

4 cm

4 cm

$6\frac{7}{10}$cm

b.

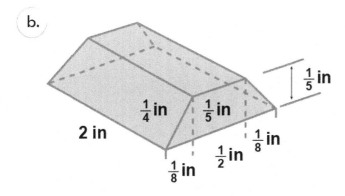

2 in

$\frac{1}{4}$ in

$\frac{1}{5}$ in

$\frac{1}{5}$ in

$\frac{1}{8}$ in

$\frac{1}{2}$ in

$\frac{1}{8}$ in

$\frac{1}{8}$ in

prepaze

Answer the following word problems:

a. Archies Arch is an interior designing firm. The following diagram is of a new kitchen countertop they designed. Approximately how many square feet of counter space is there?

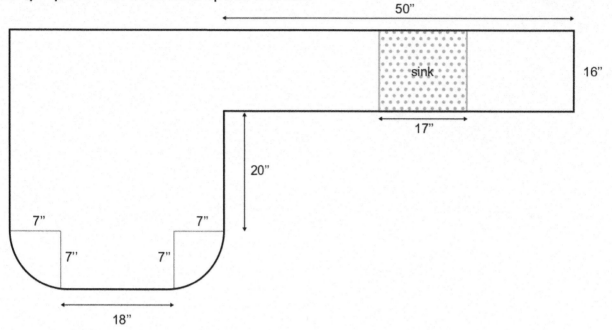

b. Phoebe is gift wrapping some glass cans that are 8 ½ inches high and 4 inches in diameter. She has a roll of paper that is 8 ½ inches wide and 60 ft long. How many cans will her paper wrap?

c. Sage built a little play toy for her kitten. She cut out two square holes with a side length of 5 cm. Determine the surface area cutting out the two square holes.

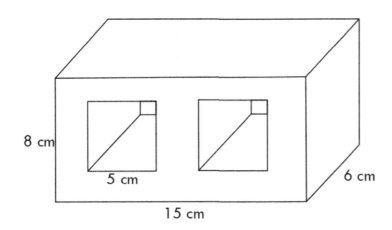

Create an area model for each product. Use the area model to write an equivalent expression that represents the area.

a. (x + 1) (x + 2)	b. (x + 3) (x + 4)
c. (x - 3) (x + 3)	d. (5 - 3) (5 + 3)

Statistics and Probability

A chance experiment consists of observing a single outcome of a chance process. A chance process is any process that is repeatable and results in one of two or more well-defined outcomes each time it is repeated. The act of performing the process and producing a result is called a trial. In a chance process, trials are independent from each other in that the result of one trial does not influence the result of any other trial. In the context of probability, observing a single outcome of a chance process is sometimes called a chance experiment

A population is any entire collection of people, animals, plants, or things that someone is interested in learning about. Each person or object in the population is called a member.

The probability of an event is a number between 0 and 1 that measures the chance that the event will occur. A probability model is a mathematical representation of a chance process defined by its sample space, events within the sample space, and the assignment of a probability for each and every event.

A random sample of size n is a sample that is selected using a process that ensures that every different possible sample of size n had the same chance of being selected as the sample. This selection process implies that every individual member of the population has the same chance of being included in the sample.

Random Sampling

An internet provider company is planning to increase the strength of its wi-fi depending on the number of electronics used in the 44 houses in the neighborhood. They conducted a survey and the results are shown as below:

Number of Electronics Used	1	2	3	4	5	6	7
Count	2	5	10	15	8	3	1

a. What is the probability that a randomly selected house uses 5 electronic gadgets?

b. What is the probability that a randomly selected house uses less than 4 electronic gadgets?

c. Complete the probability distribution table

Number of Electronics Used	1	2	3	4	5	6	7
Probability	0.045	0.114					

Biased or Unbiased

Do you think the following samples will provide valid estimates? Say if the samples are biased or unbiased and explain your reasoning:

a. To find the average hours an American family spends on television, 1000 New Yorkers were interviewed.

b. To find which seasonal vegetable was a crowd favorite, the first 500 customers to the farmer's market were interviewed.

c. To find the number of students who will be attending the school fair, all the seventh graders were surveyed.

d. To find which genre of books was the most popular in the library, 350 random visitors to the library were surveyed.

How can you improve the following surveys?

a. John conducted a survey to find out the favorite lunch of his class. His class has 43 students. He checked the lunch boxes of 10 boys in his class. As 7 of them had bought sandwiches, he concluded that sandwich was the favorite lunch of his class. How can we improve his survey to yield better results?

b. To check if the students have done well in a class test, the teacher checks the answer sheets of the top 4 kids and concludes that everyone has performed well. How can the teacher improve his survey to yield better results?

What would you choose?

a. The Art Center wants to decide on what art class the students in the primary schools in the area would prefer? What should the Art Center do?

- ◯ Interview students from different primary schools.

- ◯ Interview the parents whose kids are currently in primary schools.

- ◯ Interview all the members of the Art Center.

b. Steve asked all the boys in the basketball team "Do you like Reading?" 56% of them said "yes." Which of the following statements is true?

- ◯ 56% of all the boys in the school like Reading.

- ◯ 56% of the students in the school like Reading.

- ◯ 56% of all the boys in the Basketball team like Reading.

prepaze

Make Inferences

Make inferences from random samples by solving the following:

a.

Ava interviewed 80 members of her school for their favorite pet animal.

36 of them said they liked dogs.

The total number of students in the school is 2342.

Based on the survey, can you estimate the number of students in the entire school who like dogs?

b.

Emma's bakery wanted to find out which flavor of their cupcakes was the most bought?

They surveyed the bills randomly and found that 86 chocolate cupcakes had been sold out of the total 154 cupcakes.

What could be the estimate of chocolate cupcakes sold when the bakery reaches 1000 customers?

The management of a popular airways wanted to find out if their domestic passengers would be interested in paid movies. They interviewed passengers of 4 different flight routes to find out the preference.

The number of passengers in each flight is as shown below.

Flights	Number of Passengers
1. LA to New York	560
2. Boston to Chicago	486
3. Austin to Philadelphia	387
4. New York to Miami	890

Since all the passengers cannot be interviewed, the management decided to interview a set of people from each flight.

The management wants to take into account the preferences of all the passengers and make an unbiased decision. Can you help them by estimating how many members from each flight should they interview?

Solve the following:

a. A bird sanctuary tied a band on one of the legs of 54 red-tailed parrots and released them. A few months later, they caught 270 red tailed parrots and 48 of them had bands. Can you estimate the population of the red tailed parrots in the sanctuary?

b. 35 monkeys were released into the forest after tagging them. A few years later, the researchers found 350 monkeys. Out of the 350, 14 had tags on them. What could be the population of monkeys in the forest?

Match

Match the following:

If 2 out of the 150 milk cans is spoilt, how many cans can we expect to be spoilt in 300 milk cans?	230
16 kids in a sample of 200 prefer the beach to park. How many kids will prefer the beach in a population of 4000 kids?	4
If 23 members in a library out of 75 prefer fiction, how many members may prefer fiction in a group of 750?	160
Out of the 45 women interviewed, 12 said that they did not like black colored bags. How many women would not prefer black bags in a population of 600?	320

prepaze

Predict Who Will Win?

Grade 7 students are having an election to decide a grade representative. Toby and Sara are contesting in the election.

About the election:

- *There are 610 students in grade 7 and every one will cast their vote.*

- *A candidate who gets more than 50% of the votes will win the election.*

Mikela is trying to predict which candidate will win. Since she cannot interview all the 610 students, she will be selecting a sample of 50 students and interviewing them.

Suggest how Mikela can select a fair sample of 50 students out of the 610?

Out of the 50 students sample, 23 say that they will vote for Toby? Is this a good estimate to predict that Toby will win the actual election? Explain your answer.

Jenny wanted to determine the average height of the kids in her class. There are 38 kids in her class.

She has selected a sample of 10 students in her class randomly and recorded their heights(in inches) as below:

61, 63, 65, 61, 67, 62, 65, 64, 62, 61

a. Calculate the sample mean of the data above.

b. If she selects another 10 students for the survey, will the sample mean remain the same? Explain your reasoning.

c. If she adds two more random students to her sample with heights 63 and 61, will the sample mean change? What will the sample mean be now?

Reading hours of five friends at a book club are 2 hours, 3 hours, 2 hours, $\frac{1}{2}$ an hour, and 3 hours respectively. When a new member joined the club the mean increased by 0.2 hour. What is the reading time of the new member?

Mary scored 73, 81, 84 marks in the last three cycle tests. What score in the 4th cycle test would earn her an average of 80 for the academic year?

The age of the employees in a departmental store is as below.

Name of the employee	Age
Mark	24
Bright	28
Micheal	20
Peter	23
Allen	20
George	24
Pinto	25
Chris	20

a. What is the mean age of the group?

b. How many employees have the same age as the mean age? Name them.

c. How many employees are older than mean age and how many are younger? Name them.

Older than mean age -

Younger than mean age -

d. What is the median for the data?

prepaze

Peter's Average Goalscore

Peter, a footballer, played 9 games this year. The number of goals his team scored is as below.

3	5	2	3	4	3	2	3	2

a. What is the average number of goals per game?

b. What is the median of the data? In how many games the goals exceeded median value.

c. What is the most common number of goals?

prepaze

Manila bought some toys for her children and the prices are as below.

price ($)	number of toys
5	3
7	1
2	2
1	3
3	1

a. Find the mean value of the data.

b. Indicate the mode of the data set.

c. How many toys are priced above median value.

Alice and Holly

Alice and Holly jog every day. The distance covered by them in miles each day is as below.

Name	Monday	Tuesday	Wednesday	Thursday	Friday	Saturday
Alice	4	3.5	5	4	4.2	3
Holly	3.6	4	2.8	3.5	4	4.5

a. On an average who covers more distance?

b. What is the mean absolute deviation of Holly and Alice?

c. Who has a greater deviation?

A cosmetic company wants to compare the price of their luxury cosmetic lipsticks in their outlets of a developed country and a developing economy. They randomly selected 5 major outlets in each country and listed the prevailing price (in $).

Country	Outlet 1	Outlet 2	Outlet 3	Outlet 4	Outlet 5
Developed	20	21	20	20	18
Developing	16	14	20	18	20

a. Compare the average costs in two countries.

b. Compare the mean absolute deviation to understand the variation. Which country is more stable in pricing.

Probability Models

Read the diagram below and answer the questions.

```
    1   0
  6         2
  3         5
    7   4
```

When spinning the wheel,

a. What is the probability of landing in 0?

b. What is the probability of landing on multiples of 2?

c. What is the probability of landing in an odd number?

d. What is the probability of landing on multiples of 3?

Read the following.

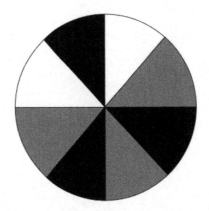

On the spinning wheel,

a. What probability that the wheel lands on black?

b. What probability that the wheel lands on black or grey?

c. What is the chance of landing on the colors other than black?

A jar has 3 red, 5 blue and 2 green marbles. On random pick

a. What is the chance of picking a green marble?

b. What is the chance of picking a red marble?

c. Which is most likely?

d. Which is least likely?

Probability of Picking a Vowel

E F G H I is a set of alphabet, if one letter is picked at random 20 times how many times the probability of picking a vowel.

Read the following and answer the chance of the event. Explain whether events are dependent or independent.

a. A coin flipped twice. Chance of getting heads both the time.

b. A dice rolled thrice, chance of getting an even number all the three time.

c. A bag has 2 pink and 3 red balls. Chance of taking a red ball first and then a pink ball without replacement.

d. Three cards 1,2,3 kept on the table. Chance of picking a 3 and then 1 without putting back the card 3 is.

Ariel Goes Shopping

There are four routes, A B C D, from Ariel's home to the shop. She takes different routes while going to the shop and coming back home.

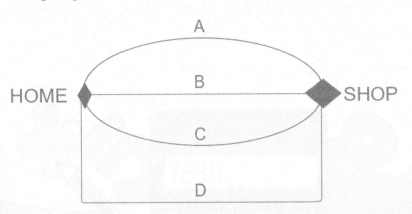

a. What is the probability that she takes Route A while going to the shop and route C while coming back?

b. What is the probability that if Route B is blocked, she uses Route C while going to the shop and route D while coming back?

Penny, Dime, and Nickel

A jar of 240 coins has pennies, dimes, and nickels in the ratio 5:8:3.

a. Probability of picking a quarter is

b. Probability of picking a dime

c. Probability of picking a nickel is

Science

Help your children learn and enjoy a wide range of information and fun facts that will surprise and amaze them. Find numerous Science experiments, cool facts, activities, and quizzes for the children to enjoy learning.

Physical Sciences

Cell Biology

A **cell** is the fundamental, structural, and functional unit of life. It is the smallest unit that can carry out all the activities of life.

Based on the number of cells they have, organisms can be classified as shown below.

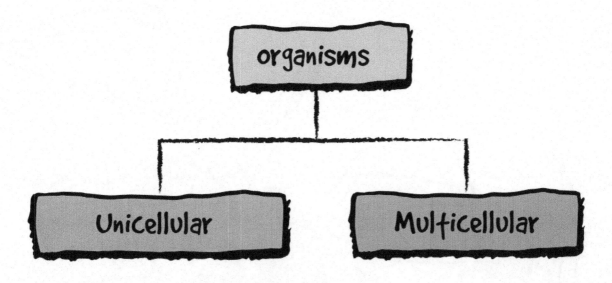

All living things like plants and animals, including humans, have cells. However, the cell that plants have is different from those of animals.

Plant and Animal cell

Label the parts of the plant cell and animal cell.

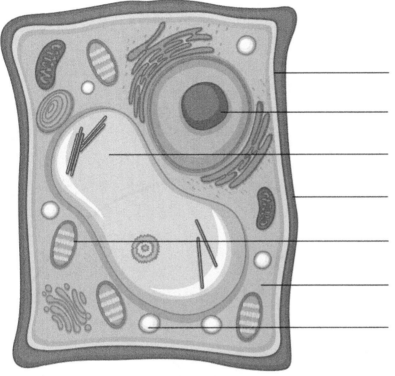

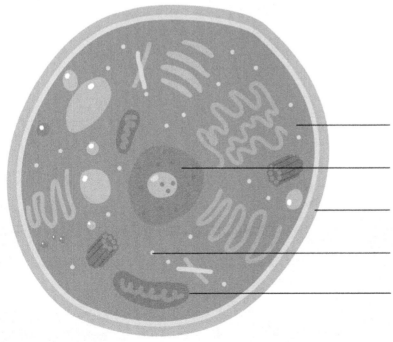

Similarities between Plant and Animal cell

Complete the venn diagram with cell organelles that are exclusive and common to plant and animal cells using the list given.

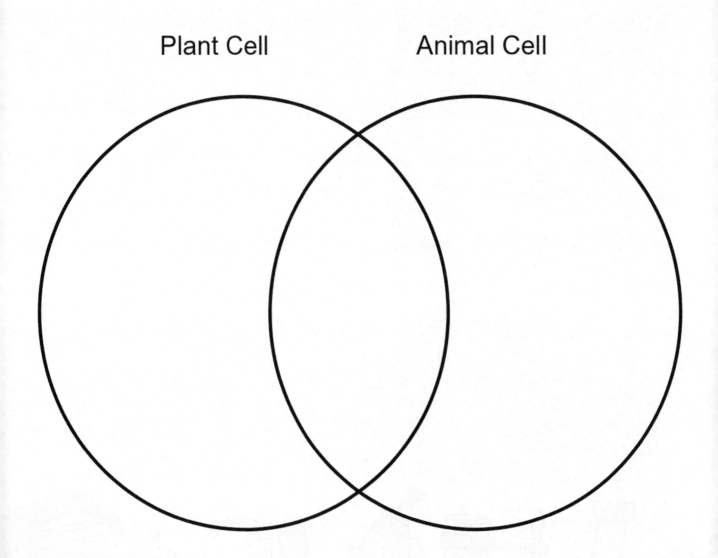

Plant Cell   Animal Cell

Cell wall	Small vacuoles	Mitochondria	Large vacuoles
Nucleus	Cytoplasm	Cell membrane	Flagella
Chloroplast	Centrioles	Golgi apparatus	Endoplasmic Reticulum

Types of cells

All cells have organelles, cell membranes, cytoplasm, and DNA. Yet, there are two basic types of cells as shown below.

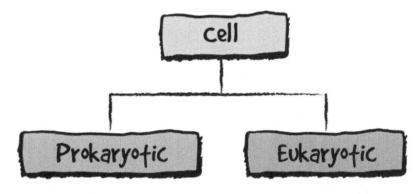

Prokaryotic	a cell that has no true nucleus
Eukaryotic	a cell that has a nucleus

Prokaryotes are usually unicellular organisms. Though nucleus is absent, they have DNA.

Though microscopic, **eukaryotes** are the largest cells. They are about 10 times the size of prokaryotes.

Eukaryotes Vs Prokaryotes

Label the parts in a prokaryotic
and eukaryotic cell.

PROKARYOTE

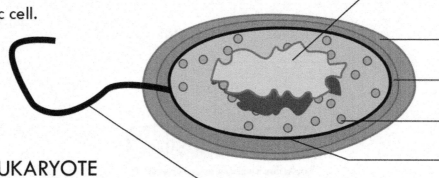

EUKARYOTE

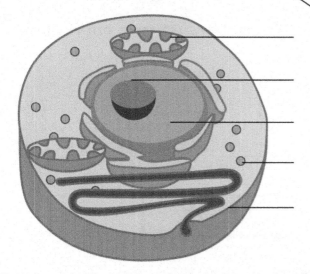

Compare and contrast the two types of cells. Use the images for reference, if necessary.

Eukaryote	Prokaryote

prepaze

Cell Organelles

Match the cell organelles with their functions.

No	Organelles	Functions
1	Cell membrane	provides shape and structure
2	Cell wall	controls cell functions
3	Flagella	makes lipids and proteins
4	Nucleus	stores water and substances
5	Ribosome	stores and controls movement of molecules made by the ER
6	Endoplasmic reticulum	regulates movement of substances in and out the cell
7	Mitochondria	helps in movement
8	Vacuole	produces protein
9	Chloroplast	releases energy
10	Golgi apparatus	makes food for the plant cell

Cellular Respiration - Crossword

Complete the crossword.

Across:

1. Ultimate source of energy for terrestrial organisms

6. Fluid filled part of a chloroplast

7. $C_6H_{12}O^6$

9. Main product of cell respiration

10. Final electron acceptor in the electron transport chain

11. One of the waste products of cell respiration

13. Molecular machine making ATP, spins

14. Second stage of cell respiration

16. Light independent reactions

17. Name of a green disk

18. Large main part of a plant which is a site of photosynthesis

19. Color of chlorophyll A

Down:

2. Stacks of disks in chloroplast

3. Structure in which photosynthesis occurs

4. These molecules are split by light to produce oxygen during photosynthesis

5. Cellular organelles in which respiration occurs

7. First stage of cell respiration

8. Green photosynthetic pigment

12. Plants convert light energy into this energy

15. Negatively charged subatomic particle

Cell Division

Mitosis	a process of cell division that forms two nuclei from the parent nucleus in eukaryotic cells
Cytokinesis	division of cytoplasm and other organelles during mitosis

Sequence the different stages of mitosis.

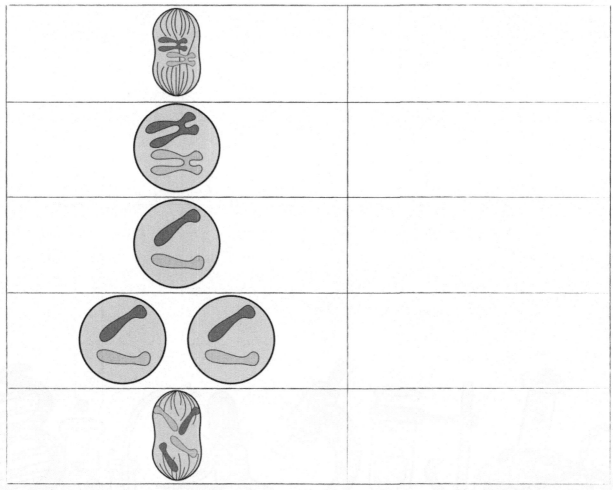

prepaze

Redraw in the correct sequence here with appropriate labels.

prepaze

Stages of Mitosis

Match the terms to the description.

A. Prophase	B. Interphase	C. Telophase	D. Metaphase	E. Anaphase

1. The sister chromatids are moving apart.	
2. The nucleolus begins to fade from view.	
3. A new nuclear membrane is forming around the chromosomes.	
4. The cytoplasm of the cell is being divided.	
5. The chromosomes become invisible.	
6. The chromosomes are located at the equator of the cell.	
7. The nuclear membrane begins to fade from view.	
8. The cleavage (division furrow) appears.	
9. The chromosomes are moving toward the poles of the cell.	
10. Chromatids line up along the equator.	
11. The spindle is formed.	
12. Chromosomes are not visible.	
13. Cytokinesis is completed.	
14. The cell plate is formed.	
15. Chromosomes are replicated.	
16. The reverse of prophase.	
17. The organization phase.	
18. The last phase where the chromatids are together.	

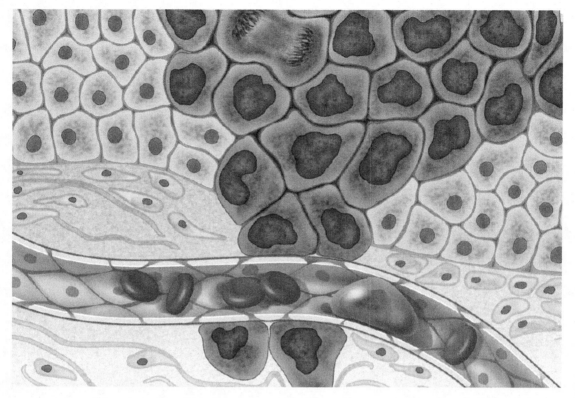

During Interphase, the parent cells replicate their chromosomes and organelles. These functions are controlled by proteins.

A cell's DNA has the information needed to make these proteins. If and when the DNA is altered, that information may be lost. Thus, there is not enough protein to control the cell division. Cells rapidly divide and form lumps called tumours.

These lumps when they affect the functioning of an organ, causes cancer.

There are more than a hundred types of cancer, usually depending on the affected organ.

Normal Cell Vs Cancerous Cell

Observe the image given. Compare the structure and organelles of a normal cell and a cancerous cell.

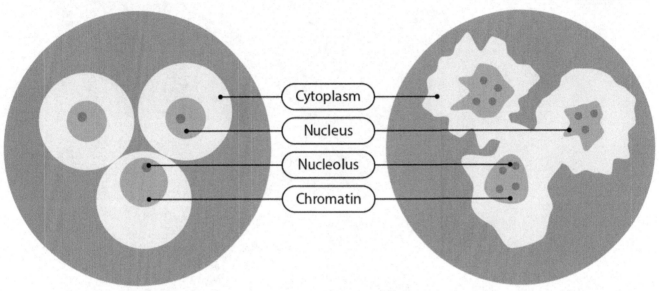

Cytoplasm

Nucleus

Nucleolus

Chromatin

Normal Cell	Cancerous Cell

How Do Cells Obtain Energy?

Answer the following questions.

1. During photosynthesis, plants take in _____ from air.

2. Fermentation is the process of breaking down sugar to form carbon dioxide and _____ .

3. Photosynthesis happens in the _____ in the leaves of plants.

4. The ability to do work is called _____ .

5. Plants use the energy from the Sun to produce oxygen and _____ .

6. Plants breakdown sugar to release energy during _____ .

7. Plants prepare their own food by the process of _____ .

8. The process in which energy is released from food in the absence of oxygen is called _____ .

9. Observe the given diagram and answer the questions that follow.

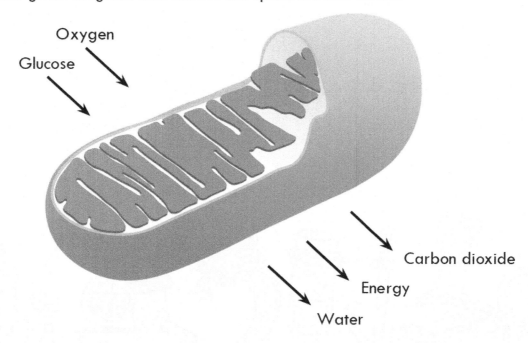

Oxygen

Glucose

Carbon dioxide

Energy

Water

a. What is the organelle shown?

b. What is the process depicted here?

c. Identify the reactants.

d. Identify the product and the byproducts.

 Make a Mummy!

Let's perform an activity to make mummies at home.

What you need:

- Meat hot dog
- A piece of string - about 10 cm in length
- Ruler
- 4 pairs of disposable gloves
- 4 paper towels

- Kitchen scale
- Airtight storage box - bigger than the hot dog
- Baking Soda - enough to fill the box thrice

What to do:

 **Step 1** — Spread a paper towel on the working surface. Measure the length of the hot dog and make a note of it in the table given below this activity.

Step 2 — Use the piece of string to measure the circumference of the hot dog. Make note of this in the table.

 **Step 3** — Measure the weight of the hot dog using the kitchen scale and write it down in the given table.

 **Step 4** — Now to begin with the mummification. Spread baking soda for at least 2 cm at the base of the airtight box. Choose to use from a new sealed box. Using baking soda already left in the open will not help in this activity.

Step 5

Lay the hot dog on top of the 2-centimeter baking soda layer in the box.

Step 6

Cover the hot dog with baking soda for about 2 cm again on top of it. Fill the sides too. The hot dog should be completely covered by baking soda.

Step 7

Cover the box with the lid to make it airtight. Place the setup in a shady place. Let it stay for a week.

Step 8

After a week, wear a different set of gloves. Check on your hot dog. Gently tap to remove all the baking soda. Repeat Steps 1 to 3. Record your measurements in the next row.

Step 9

Observe the hot dog. What changes do you observe? Is the color any different? Does it smell? Record your observations in the comment section.

Step 10

Discard the used baking soda. With a fresh batch of baking soda repeat Steps 4 to 7. Let it stay for another week.

Step 11

Record your observations. Repeat Steps 8 to 10. Let it stay for another week. The process happens for a total of 21 days with 3 batches of baking soda.

Step 12

Plot your readings on three different graphs to show changes in - length, circumference, and weight of the hotdog through the 3 weeks of mummification.

Date	Length in cm	Circumference in cm	Weight in g	Comments

Plot graphs with the collected data.

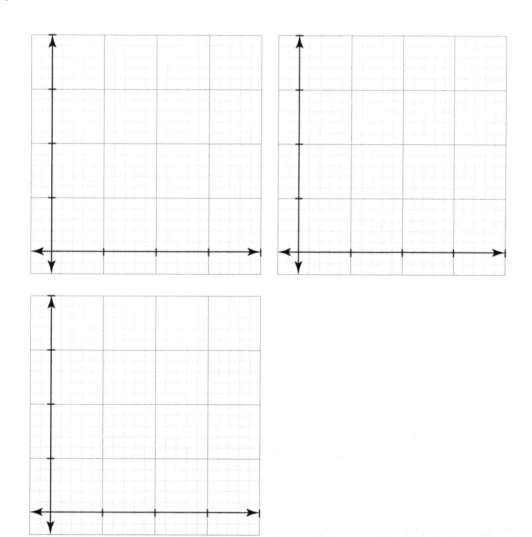

Investigating Reproduction

What are the advantages and disadvantages of sexual and asexual reproduction?

1. Why do you think bacteria, plants, and many other organisms reproduce faster than humans?

_____

_____

_____

_____

2. Why do you think humans do not reproduce asexually?

_____

_____

_____

_____

3. Name 5 organisms that reproduce sexually and 5 organisms that reproduce asexually.

Sexual reproduction	Asexual reproduction

4. Assume the role of an ecologist. Study the methods of reproduction in organisms listed above. Fill in the table with information you have gathered about the methods of reproduction.

	Sexual reproduction	Asexual reproduction
Complexity of the organisms (including size)		
Cell division		
Number of parents that contribute genetic information to the offspring		

Reproductive mechanisms		
Amount of parental care involved		
Possibility of genetic variation in the offspring		
Time taken		
Number of offsprings		
Advantages		

Identify and explain each stage of meiosis.

Stage of meiosis	Explanation

Mitosis Vs Meiosis in Humans

Compare and contrast mitosis and meiosis in the human body.

	Mitosis	Meiosis
Function		
Types of cells that undergo this process		
Location in the human body		
Number of parent cells involved		
Number of daughter cells produced		
Size of daughter cells as compared to parent cells		
Change in the number of chromosomes		
Number of divisions in the nucleus		
Difference between the DNAs of mother cell and daughter cells		
Type of reproduction		

DNA

Deoxyribonucleic Acid (DNA) is a molecule that encodes the genetic instructions used in the development and functioning of all organisms. It is made up of subunits called nucleotides. A nucleotide consists of a sugar, a phosphate, and a base.

There are four types of bases as shown below.

Bases of Nucleotide

- Adenine
- Thymine
- Guanine
- Cytosine

DNA Molecule

Label the parts of a DNA molecule.

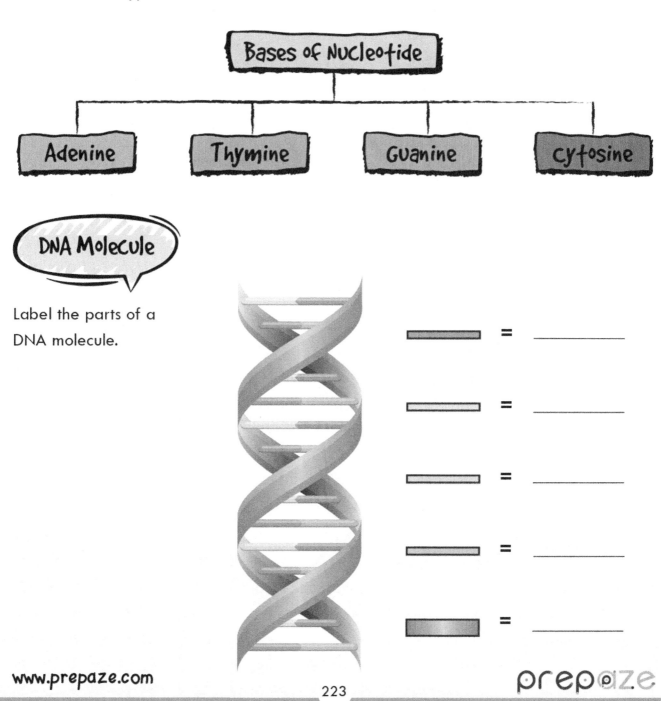

▭ = _____

▭ = _____

▭ = _____

▭ = _____

▭ = _____

Want to See Some Real DNA?

Let's do a simple experiment to separate DNA from onion.

What you need:

- An adult lab assistant
- An onion
- Knife
- Cutting board
- Blender
- Salt
- A strainer
- Dishwashing liquid or clear shampoo

- 2 glasses
- 2 spoons
- A chopstick
- Meat tenderizer
- Rubbing alcohol - look for more than 70%, in supermarkets
- An apron

Safety Warning:

1. Rubbing alcohol is poisonous. Don't take it anywhere near your face. Ensure to wash all the kitchen utensils and your hands well after the activity.

2. Do not put your hand into the blender. The blades are sharp.

3. Request an adult to stay by you throughout the activity. Seek help wherever needed.

What to do:

Step 1 Wear the apron. Chop the onion and put in the blender.

Step 2 Add water twice as much the onion and 1 teaspoon of salt. Blend to a mushy consistency.

Step 3 Label one glass as "Control" and leave it undisturbed. The explanation and purpose of a control is explained below.

Step 4 Label the other glass as "DNA extraction."

Step 5 Place the two glasses on a flat surface. Pass the blended mixture through the strainer to filter it. Then, fill upto one-third of each glass.

Step 6 Add dishwashing liquid - one-sixth the amount of onion juice in the "DNA extraction" glass. Do not add any to the "control" glass.

Step 7 Step 7: Add 0.5 teaspoon of meat tenderizer to the "DNA extraction" glass.

Step 8 Insert a spoon into each of the glasses and stir gently. Let it sit for 10 minutes.

Step 9 Very slowly add rubbing alcohol to each of the glasses. The amount of alcohol must be the same as the amount of mixture in the glass.

Step 10 You will notice alcohol being lighter, floats above the mixture in the glass.

 In a few minutes, stringy globs will appear in the "DNA extraction" glass, making your activity a success. The strings thus separated are the DNA of onion.

 Use the chopstick to slowly swirl the strings through the DNA and lift them up for a closer look. Use touch and feel the DNA strands with your fingers. Remember to wash your hands thoroughly afterward.

 Check the "control" glass. How is the mixture different from the one in "DNA extraction" glass?

Science of extracting DNA

DNA is present in the nucleus of every organism. Dissolving the cell walls helps in the release of DNA. A DNA molecule is long and string-like. However, a single DNA molecule is too small to be seen with naked eye. But when enough of those strands tangle together, and form a blob, it can be held. These clumps of DNA from onion are pale and feel slimy.

The "Control"

The activity calls for extraction of DNA in only one glass.

Why did we use two?

The glass that has onion juice with no additives is called the **control**. Scientists never perform an experiment without a control for comparison.

What is it used for?

Usually, once the experiment is done and you see a blob floating, how will you ensure it is DNA and not just pieces of onion? A control gives you something to compare with. It helps you identify the changes that have happened through the experiment.

prepaze

Extended Learning:

Make a record of your observations.

1. Repeat activity with other vegetables like broccoli, spinach, and bananas.

2. What do you think will happen if you do not use a meat tenderizer?

3. What happens if you use a cloth as a filter instead of a strainer?

What the extracted DNA would look like?

Reinforcement: Genetics

Answer the following questions.

1. Identify if each of the following genotypes are homozygous or heterozygous.

a. RR - _____

b. Bb - _____

c. TT - _____

d. FF - _____

e. Cc - _____

2. Complete the following definitions of some basic terms in genetics.

a. Genotype is the _____ makeup represented by _____ .

b. Phenotype is the _____ appearance of a trait.

c. Purebred - also called _____ consists of gene pairs with _____ genes.

d. Hybrid - also called _____ consists of gene pairs with _____ genes.

3. Determine the phenotype for each genotype using the information provided.

a. Tall (T) is dominant to short (t)

i. TT - _____

ii. Tt - _____

iii. tt - _____

prepaze

b. Black hair (B) is dominant to blonde (b)

i. BB - _____

ii. Bb - _____

iii. bb - _____

4. Complete the Punnett squares for a homozygous, tall father and a heterozygous, tall mother and answer the questions that follow.

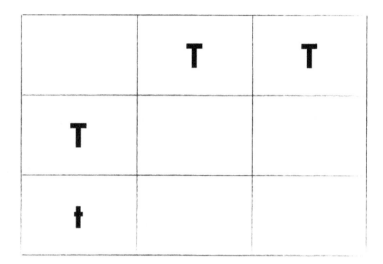

a. What are the chances of a child being tall?

_____ %

b. What are the chances of a child being short?

_____ %

Monster Genetics

What if monsters had genetic codes? Read the given data and answer the questions that follow.

Mike

Genotype	Phenotype
Gg	Green body color
ee	One eye
CC	Clawed toes
Ff	Four fingers

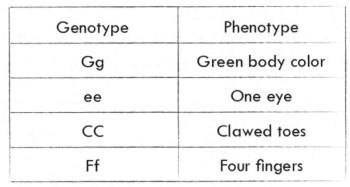

G - green body color   C - clawed toes

g - yellow body color   c - no claws

E - two eyes   F - four fingers

e - one eye   f - five fingers

Sully

Genotype	Phenotype
Pp	Blue-purple body color
Hh	Horned ears
bb	Blue eyes
LL	Long hair

P - purple body color,   B - red eyes

co-dominant   b - blue eyes

p - blue body color   L - long hair

H - horned ears   l - short hair

h - no horns

1. Which of Sully's traits are heterozygous?

2. Which of Sully's traits are homozygous recessive?

3. Which of Mike's traits are heterozygous dominant?

4. Draw and color the monsters with the given genotypes.

gg/Ee/Cc/ff	pp/hh/Bb/ll

5. For each phenotype of monsters of Mike's species, list the possible genotypes.

Phenotype	Genotype(s)
Green body color	
Yellow body color	
Two eyes	
One eye	
No claws	
Five fingers	

6. Draw Mike's parents with the given genotypes.

a. Mother: gg - Ee - Cc - ff

b. Father: Gg - Ee - cc - Ff

Mike's mother	Mike's father

prepaze

7. a. How many eyes does Mike's father have?

b. How many eyes does Mike's mother have?

c. Explain how Mike is one-eyed?

_____

_____

_____

_____

_____

8. Complete the Punnett squares to show the possible genotypes of body color for Sulley and his siblings. What are the possible body color phenotypes, and the probability for each phenotype?

	P	p
P		
p		

_____

_____

_____

_____

prepaze

Family Portrait Game

Answer the following questions to create a family portrait. Oh, and you will also need a die (plural: dice) to complete this activity.

1. SpongeBob SquarePants is the husband of SpongeSusie RoundPants. SpongeBob is heterozygous for his square shape, and SpongeSusie is round. Create a Punnett square to show the possibilities of shapes that would result if Bob and Susie had children.

a. What is the probability of a child with a square body? _____ %

b. What is the probability of a child with a round body? _____ %

2. SpongeBob is heterozygous for his yellow color, and SpongeSusie is blue. Create a Punnett square to show the possibilities of colors that would result if Bob and Susie had children.

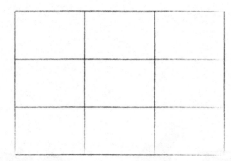

a. What is the probability of a child that is yellow? _____ %

b. What is the probability of a child that is blue? _____ %

prepaze

3. Follow instructions given here to complete questions 4 and 5.

a. Number the boxes of the Punnett squares you have created as
1, 2, 3, and 4.

b. Roll the die to determine each of the characteristics for each child.
For instance, if it lands on number 2, the child will carry the trait you
have numbered as 2 in the corresponding Punnett Square.

c. Roll again if the die lands on numbers 5 and 6.

4. Roll the dice to determine the genotype that contributes to the body
shape of each child.

a. Genotype for Child 1: _____

b. Phenotype for Child 1: _____

c. Genotype for Child 2: _____

d. Phenotype for Child 2: _____

5. Roll the dice to determine the genotype that contributes to the body color of each child.

a. Genotype for Child 1: _____

b. Phenotype for Child 1: _____

c. Genotype for Child 2: _____

d. Phenotype for Child 2: _____

6. Draw a family portrait of SpongeBob and SpongeSusie with their two children, as determined in the answers.

Bonus: Compare the family portrait you have created with your friends' and observe the similarities and differences.

Evolution

Branching Diagram

Cladistics is an approach to biological classification.

A **cladogram** is a diagram used in cladistics to show the relations among organisms. However, a cladogram is not an evolutionary tree as it does not show how ancestors are related to their descendants. It is also called a **branching diagram.**

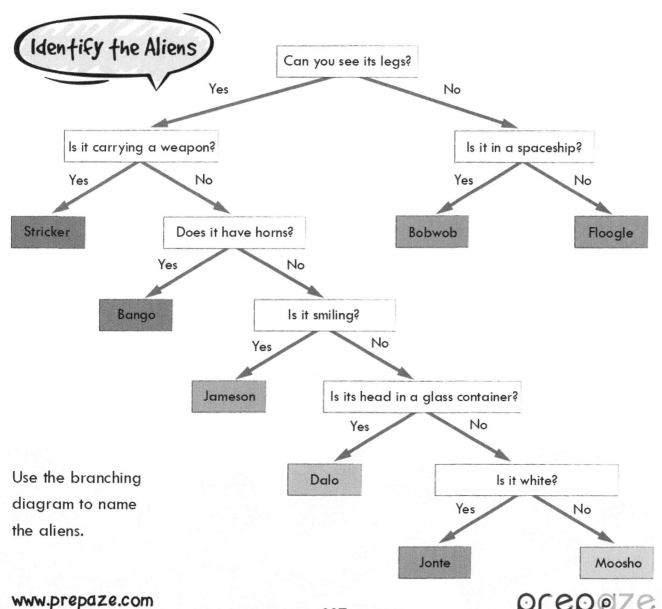

Identify the Aliens

Can you see its legs?
- Yes → Is it carrying a weapon?
  - Yes → Stricker
  - No → Does it have horns?
    - Yes → Bango
    - No → Is it smiling?
      - Yes → Jameson
      - No → Is its head in a glass container?
        - Yes → Dalo
        - No → Is it white?
          - Yes → Jonte
          - No → Moosho
- No → Is it in a spaceship?
  - Yes → Bobwob
  - No → Floogle

Use the branching diagram to name the aliens.

prepaze

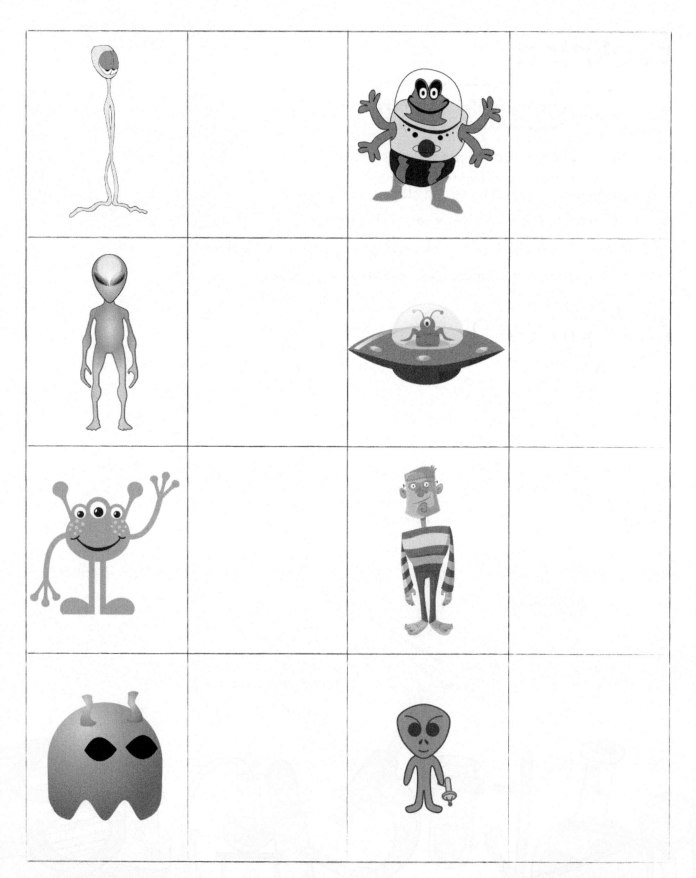

Reading a cladogram

Observe the given cladogram. Each letter represents a derived characteristic. Match the letters to the characteristics given below.

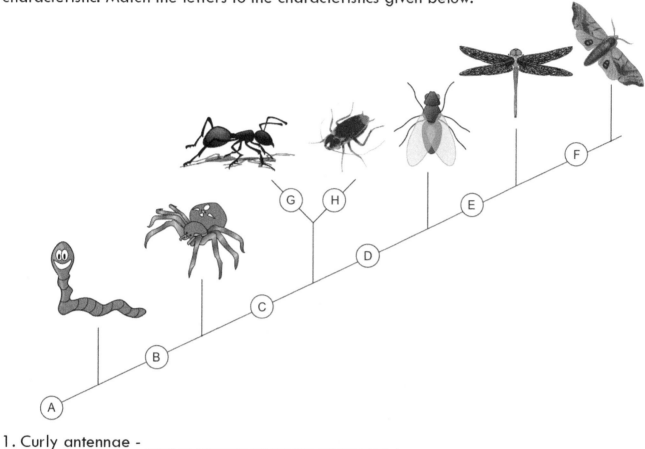

1. Curly antennae - _____

2. Crushing mouthparts - _____

3. Wings - _____

4. 6 legs - _____

5. Segmented body - _____

6. Legs - _____

7. Double set of wings - _____

8. Cerci - _____

prepaze

Fact, fiction, or opinion

Read the following sentences and say if they are facts, fiction, or opinion.

1. Humans evolved from monkeys.

2. To do a good job, it is important that scientists believe in evolution.

3. Evolution can be observed.

4. Mutations cannot create new traits.

5. There is evidence that humans and dinosaurs coexisted.

6. Humans share a common ancestor with the chimpanzees.

7. The theory of evolution has been changing since the time of Darwin.

8. Evolution should be taught in biology class.

9. The Earth is about 10,000 years old.

10. All traits are adaptations produced by natural selection.

Human Vs Chimp

Observe the skeletons of humans and chimpanzees and answer the questions that follow.

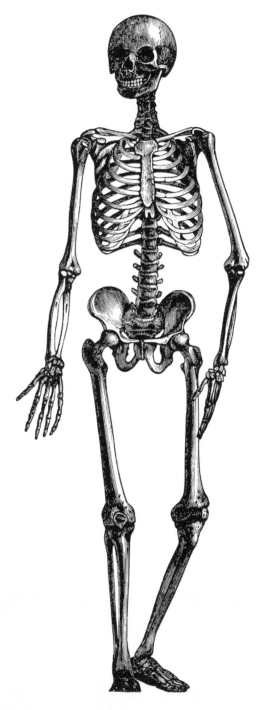

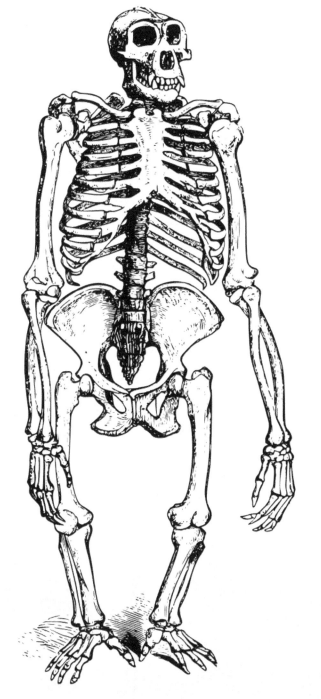

1. Circle the forelimbs, hindlimbs, and pelvic bones of the two organisms.

_____

2. Identify three similarities in the shape and size of bones in humans and chimpanzees.

_____

3. Identify three differences in the shape and size of bones in humans and chimpanzees.

_____

4. What are the forelimbs of chimpanzees adapted for?

_____

Zoo Scavenger Hunt

On your visit to a zoo, find one organism for each of the given categories. You may take pictures of the animal and the sign board that describes the animal. Use these pics to label the photos later. Fill in the second column with the names of corresponding organism(s).

1. A carnivorous bird	
2. A parasitic organism	
3. A great ape	
4. An aquatic mammal	
5. An animal that is native to Australia	

prepaze

6. A rodent	
7. An animal that lives in desert	
8. A cartilage fish	
9. An arctic animal	
10. A new world monkey	
11. A nocturnal animal	
12. A crocodilian	
13. A spider	
14. A tortoise or turtle	
15. An endangered animal	
16. An animal with its young one	
17. A flying mammal	
18. An animal that is native to Africa	
19. A flightless bird	
20. A reptile	

Note: No two answers can be the same.

Reinforcement: Evolution

Answer the following questions and complete the crossword.

Down:

1. A _____ organ is a part of the body that is functionless.

2. Structures that are similar in related organisms, like the bones in an arm.

4. The formation of new species.

6. Remains of organisms that lived in the past.

Across:

2. Offspring of two different species like a liger.

3. The famous birds studied by Darwin on the Galapagos.

5. Refers to differences among individuals in a population.

7. A diagram that shows features that are common to groups.

8. Traits that help organisms survive and reproduce.

9. A process by which evolution occurs; natural _____ .

prepaze

Earth and Life History

Rock cycle

Label the diagram of rock cycle and answer the questions that follow.

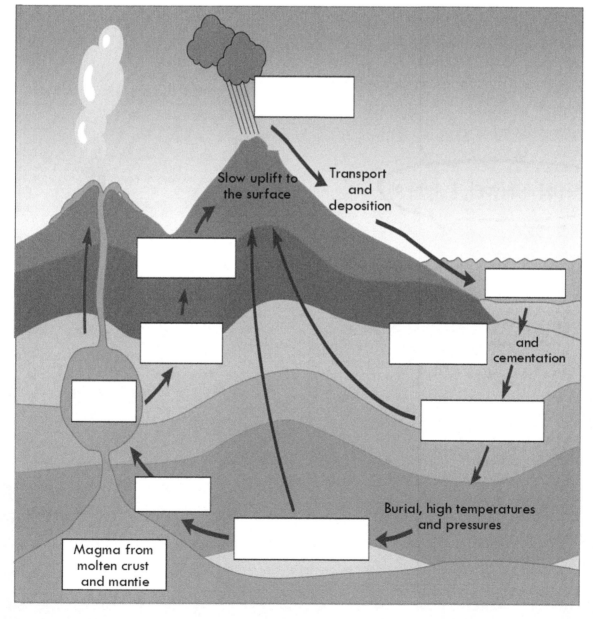

Slow uplift to the surface

Transport and deposition

and cementation

Burial, high temperatures and pressures

Magma from molten crust and mantie

1. A series of processes that slowly change rocks from one kind to another is referred to as the _____ .

2. All rocks follow the same pathway through the rock cycle is a false statement. Why?

_____

_____

_____

3. Which process changes sedimentary rocks into metamorphic rocks? _____

4. Which process changes igneous rocks into sedimentary rocks? _____

5. Which process changes magma into igneous rocks? _____

Identify the different disturbances of rock layers.

Observe the image and answer the questions that follow.

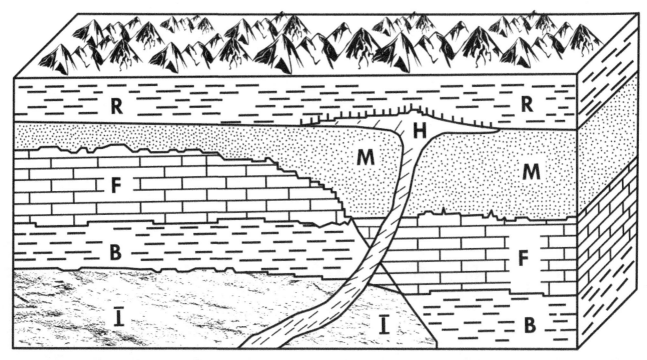

1. Arrange the rock layers from oldest to youngest relative ages.

_____

_____

2. Why are the layers of rocks on the left of the image not in line with those on the right?

_____

_____

_____

_____

3. If fossils were found in the layer F on the left side of the image, and in the layer M on the right, which one would be older? Why?

_____

_____

_____

_____

4. Which rock layer would not contain fossils? Why?

_____

_____

_____

Did You Know?

Scientists often determine the sequence of sedimentary layers based on the fossils that are found within them. The fossils are compared to decide if the two layers are from the same geologic period or one is older than the other.

Sedimentary Layers - Puzzle

Each row from A-E represents a sedimentary layer formed during a certain period. Follow instructions to reconstruct the layers of the Earth.

Step 1   Take a photocopy of the rows from A-E.

Step 2   Cut them to make strips.

Step 3   Begin by placing the oldest layer B at the bottom. Then, decide which layer will come next.

Step 4   Note: The layer that follows will have the same organisms as the older layer and some new ones too.

Step 5   Ensure that organisms do not reappear after disappearing. Continue until the layers are in order with the youngest on top. Refer to the key provided below to identify each of the organisms depicted here.

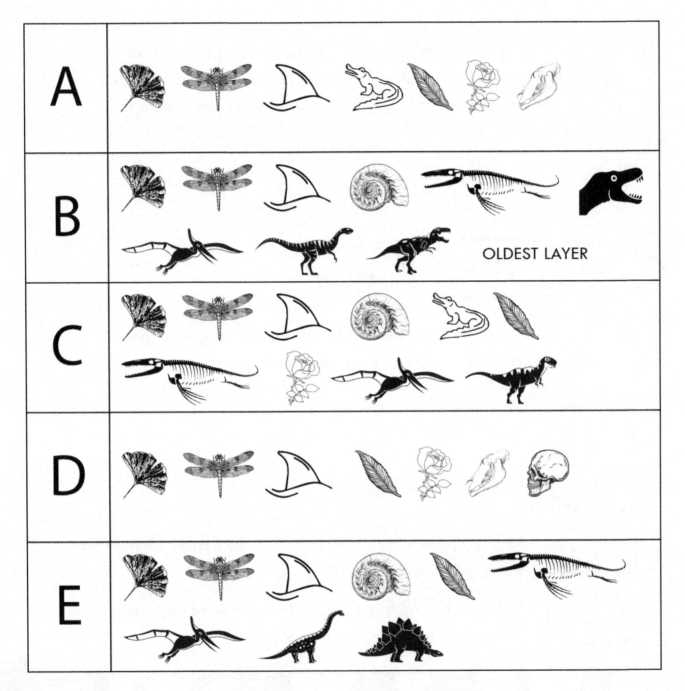

Key

	Gingko		Horse
	Dragonfly		Ichthyosaurus
	Ammonite		Stegosaurus
	Shark		Homo sapiens
	Bird		Tarbosaurus

	Flowering Plants		Seismosaurus
	Postosuchus		Pterosaurs
	Dyrosaurs		Coelophysis
		Effigia	

prepaze

Word Grid

Find the given list of words in the word grid.

B	T	J	K	C	M	N	N	K	W	N	G	B	Y	M
E	T	E	A	R	M	O	U	N	T	A	I	N	E	L
D	E	V	C	E	I	E	M	O	E	P	Q	T	Y	A
R	E	K	D	T	R	A	N	A	L	C	A	P	H	R
O	N	I	A	O	O	A	T	A	N	M	I	A	P	E
C	T	L	S	U	C	N	T	L	O	T	B	N	A	N
K	B	I	R	L	Q	E	I	R	E	F	L	G	R	I
A	O	T	O	T	S	H	P	C	G	D	C	E	G	M
N	S	V	L	X	T	H	T	M	A	G	M	A	O	T
O	O	U	F	E	I	L	E	R	O	C	P	R	P	S
A	A	C	O	C	R	E	I	C	A	L	G	I	O	U
F	V	Q	E	E	R	I	F	T	Y	E	A	D	T	R
I	G	A	Z	A	N	F	O	S	S	I	L	G	N	C
Z	D	W	L	I	N	G	L	I	O	S	N	E	D	P
Y	R	A	T	N	E	M	I	D	E	S	M	O	T	V

Ablation, Bedrock, Cave, Delta, Earthquake, Core, Crust, Erosion, Fault, Fossil, Glacier, Igneous, Lava, Magma, Mantle, Metamorphic, Mineral, Mountain, Ocean, Tide, Pangea, Tectonic, Relief, Ridge, Rift, Sedimentary, Soil, Topography, Volcano

Structure and Function in Living Systems

Scientific Taxonomy

Domain
↓
Kingdom
↓
Phylum
↓
Class
↓
Order
↓
Family
↓
Genus
↓
Species

Carolus Linnaeus, a Swedish botanist, is called the father of taxonomy.

The classification starts with one group of a variety of organisms and becomes more selective as the groups get more specific.

There are eight common groups as shown in the diagram.

Domain is the highest rank on organisms. There are three main domains - bacteria, archaea, and eukaryota. Species is the last and major taxonomic rank which are subdivided into subspecies in certain cases only.

prepaze

Vascular and Nonvascular Plants

Categorize the given characteristics as those of vascular plants and nonvascular plants.

Vascular Plants	Nonvascular Plants	Characteristics
		grow close to ground
		some have flowers or cones
		have leaves, roots, and stems
		simplest of plants
		must be near a source of water
		don't have leaves, roots, or stems
		have a system of tubes that carry water and food
		grow close to the ground

categorization of Plants

Complete the tree diagram with categories and examples of plants based on their classification.

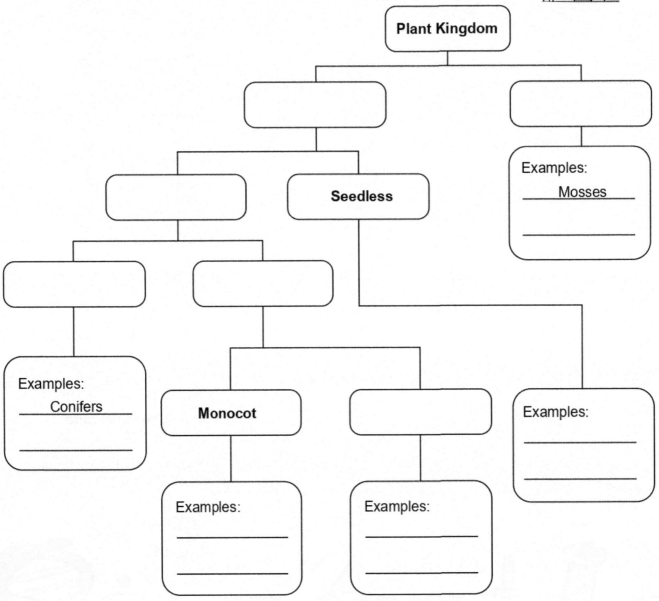

Plant Kingdom

Seedless

Examples:
___Mosses___

_____

Examples:
___Conifers___

_____

Monocot

Examples:
_____

_____

Examples:
_____

_____

Examples:
_____

_____

prepaze

Plant cell and Animal cell

Complete the crossword by answering the questions that follow about plant and animal cells.

Across:

2. Present inside the nucleus

5. Stores food and water for the cell, usually larger in plant cell than animal cell

6. The outer covering of a plant cell

8. May be found attached to endoplasmic reticulum

9. Also called the powerhouse of the cell

10. Control center of the cell

Down:

1. Processes and packages proteins and lipids in the cell

3. Contains chlorophyll

4. The outer covering of an animal cell

7. Also called suicidal bags of the cell

prepaze

Parts of a flower

Label the parts of the flower given below. Color the flower appropriately. Describe one feature of each part of the given flower in the table.

Who Am I?

Identify the different parts of a flower using the given clues. Also write the functions of the identified parts.

Clues	Part of the Flower	Functions
I am the male part of the flower. Who am I?		
I hold the anther up in a flower. Who am I?		
I am the female part of the flower. Who am I?		
I am the most colorful part of a flower. Who am I?		
I produce pollen. Who am I?		
I am the part of the flower where fertilization occurs. Who am I?		
I am usually green and support the petals as they bloom. Who am I?		
I am a tube-like structure that pollen travels through. Who am I?		

Seed Adaptations

State the method of seed dispersal for each of the seeds listed and describe the adaptations of the seed that are suited to the mechanism.

Name of the plant	Image of the seed	Seed dispersal mechanism	Adaptations
coconut			
blackberry			
dandelion			
burdock			
green peas			

prepaze

Label the parts of the male and female reproductive systems using the words from the grid given below.

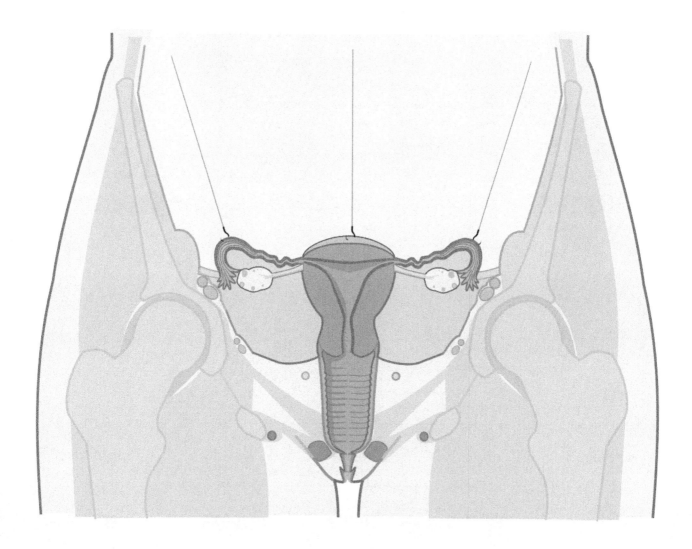

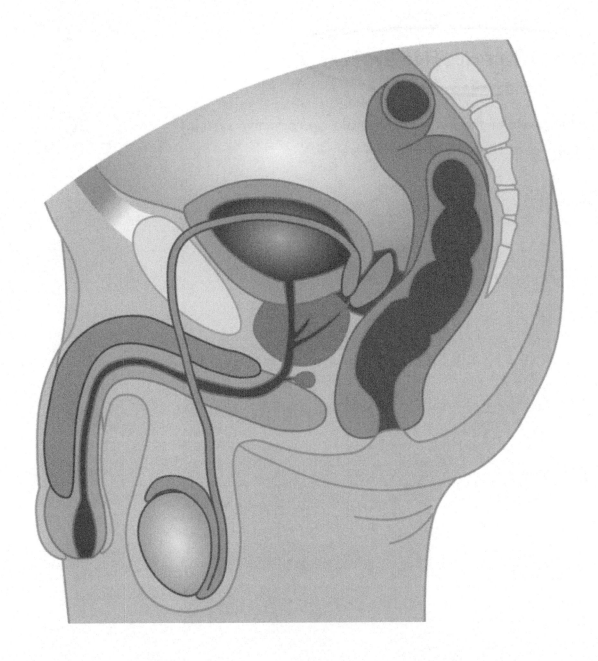

scrotum	uterus	testes	ovary	sperm duct
urethra	bladder	vagina	penis	oviduct
cervix	rectum	fallopian tubes	endometrium	anus

Gestation Period

Pregnancy in a mammal occurs when the sperm fertilizes the egg and a zygote is formed. The zygote gets implanted in the endometrium on the walls of the uterus of the female. The growth of the zygote into an embryo and then into a baby happens over a period of time. This time period from fertilization until childbirth is called the gestation period.

Find out the gestation period of each of these animals.

Animals	Gestation Period (in days)	Animals	Gestation Period (in days)
1. Dog		9. Zebra	
2. Beaver		10. Cat	
3. Giraffe		11. Chipmunk	
4. Gorilla		12. African Elephant	
5. Hamster		13. Guinea Pig	
6. Moose		14. Kangaroo	
7. Porcupine		15. Lion	
8. Wolf		16. Human	

Stages of Foetal Development

Number the stages of the foetus in order of their development.

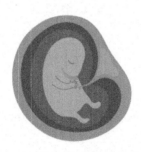

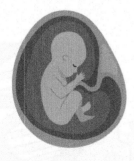

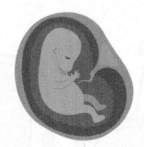

prepaze

Eyes and Ears

Match the parts of the human eye and ear, and write one of their functions in the table. Color the diagram.

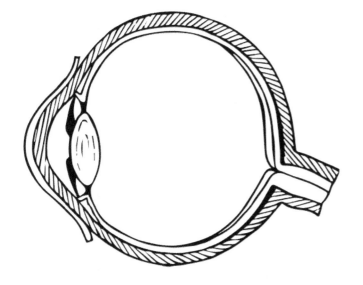

Sclera
Lens
Retina
Iris
Pupil
Cornea
Vitreous humor

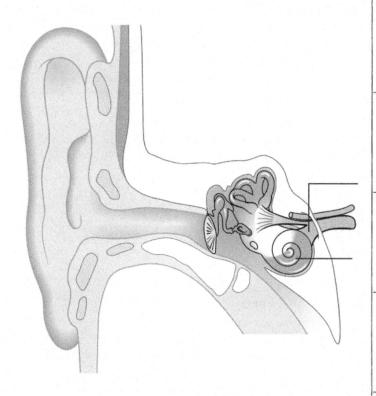

Pinna

_____

_____

Ear canal

_____

_____

Auditory nerve

_____

_____

Eustachian tube

_____

_____

Cochlea

_____

_____

Eardrum

_____

_____

Ossicles

_____

_____

Physical Principles in Living Systems

Light Travels in a Straight Line

Perform an activity to prove that light travels in a straight line.

What you need:

 A flashlight

 3 index cards

 Glue tack or double sided tape

 A ruler

 A hole puncher

 A pencil

What to do:

Step 1 — Use the ruler to draw two diagonals on the index cards. Punch a hole at the intersection of the diagonals.

Step 2 — Make the cards stand vertically, equidistant, using the glue tack. Ensure that the cards are in a straight line with their holes aligned. Place the setup in front of a wall.

Step 3 — Turn off other sources of light in the room.

Step 4 — Hold the flashlight near the first card, such that it lights up the hole on that card.

Step 5 — Notice that the light passes through the three holes and lands on the wall beyond the third card.

prepaze

 Now, move the second card slightly to your right, such that its hole is not aligned with the other two.

 Notice that the light passes through the first hole, but is stopped by the second card.
Hence, the light ray does not reach the third card.

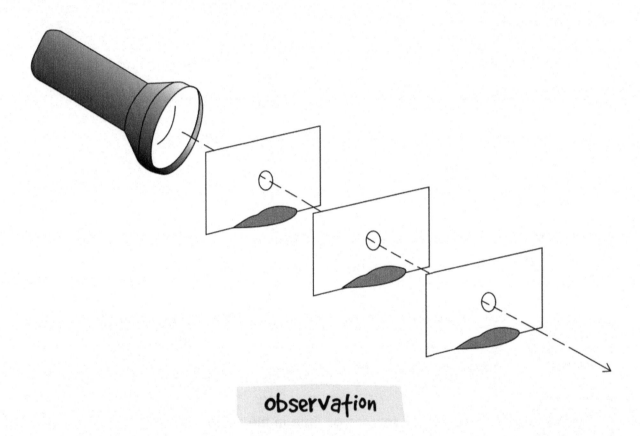

observation

a. When the three cards were aligned, the light _____ (reached/ did not reach) the wall.

b. When the three cards were not aligned, the light _____ (reached/ did not reach) the wall.

c. This shows that _____ travels in a _____ (straight/curved) line.

prepaze

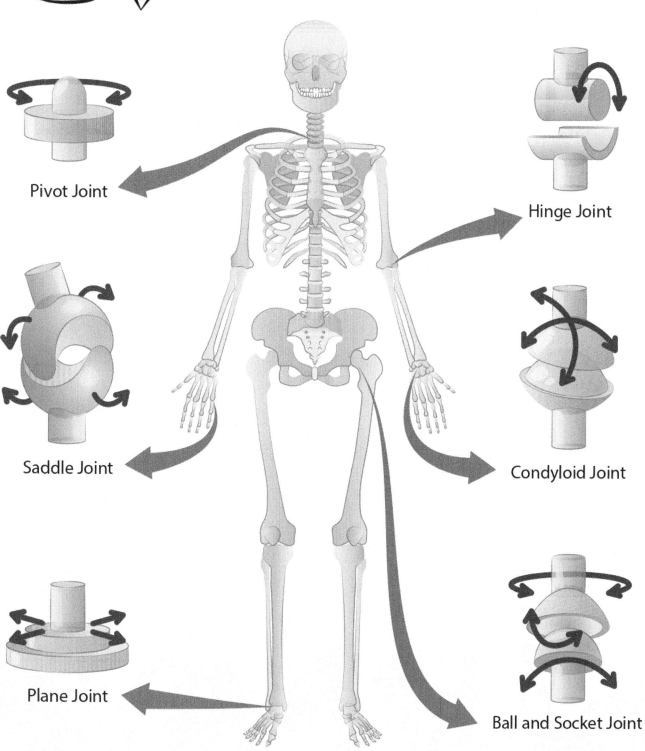

Pivot Joint

Hinge Joint

Saddle Joint

Condyloid Joint

Plane Joint

Ball and Socket Joint

Try doing the specified actions with each joint, and place a check mark if the action is possible.

Type of Joint	Part of the body	Rotation	Folding/ unfolding	Rotating	Swinging	Stretching
		☐	☐	☐	☐	☐
		☐	☐	☐	☐	☐
		☐	☐	☐	☐	☐
		☐	☐	☐	☐	☐
		☐	☐	☐	☐	☐
		☐	☐	☐	☐	☐

prepaze

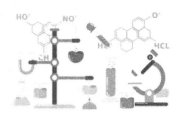

Systems in Our Body

Identify the different systems in our body. Write two purposes of each of these systems.

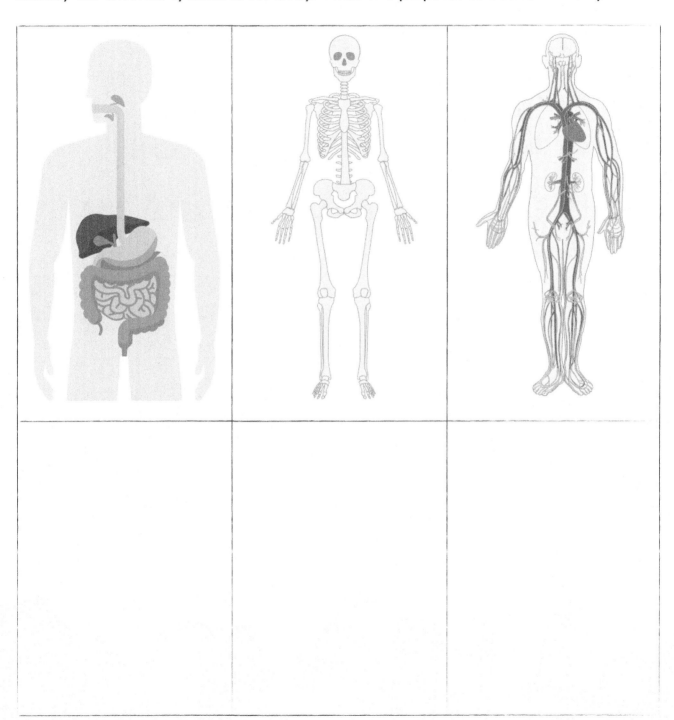

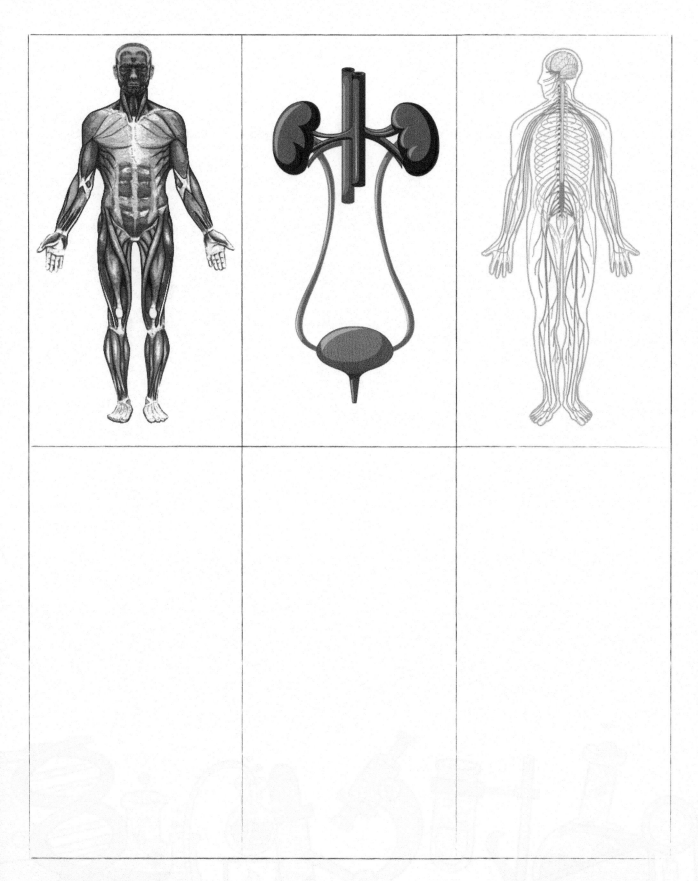

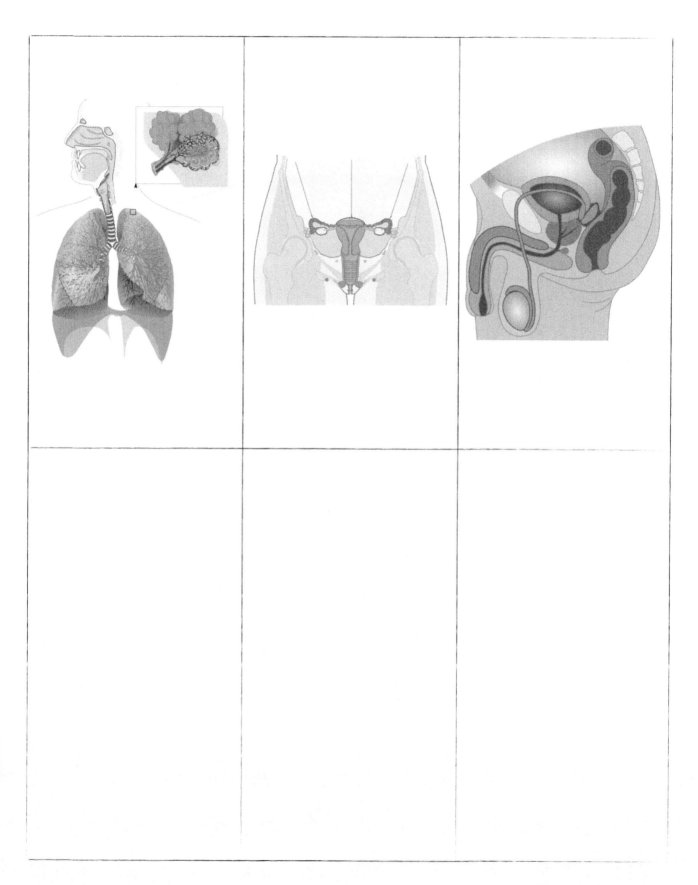

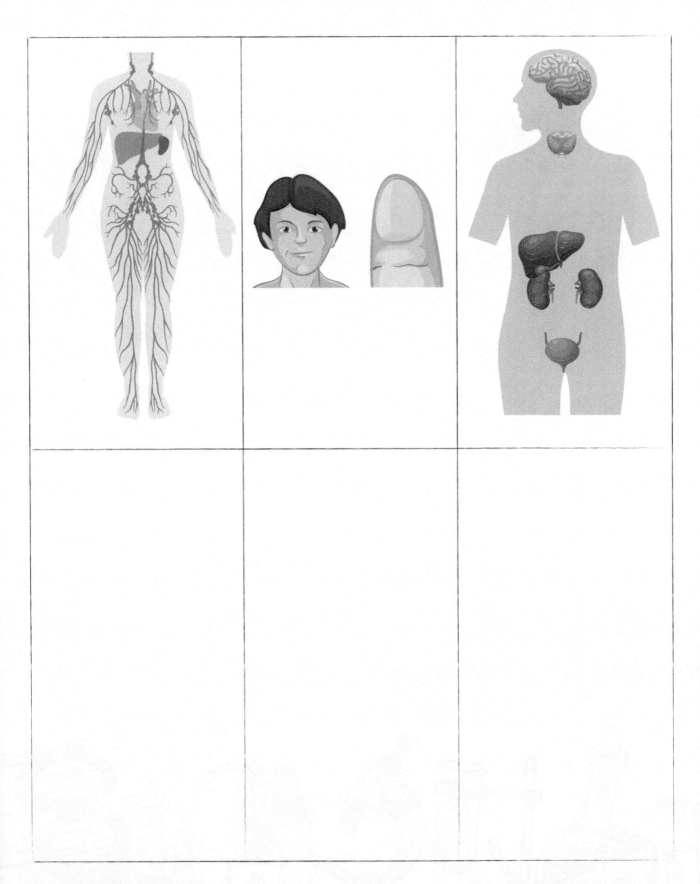

prep@ze

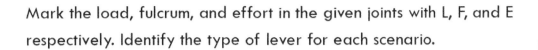

Levers in the Human Body

Mark the load, fulcrum, and effort in the given joints with L, F, and E respectively. Identify the type of lever for each scenario.

Describe the following:

1. Third-class Lever

_____

_____

2. Second-class Lever

_____

_____

3. First-class Lever

_____

Complete the diagram to define the path of blood in the human heart. Color the path of deoxygenated blood blue and the oxygenated blood red.

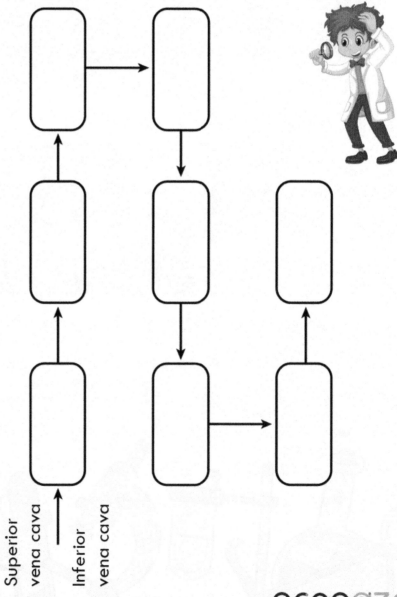

Superior vena cava

Inferior vena cava

Label the parts of the human heart and draw arrows to show the direction of the flow of the blood. Color the heart keeping in mind the color of the blood flowing through it.

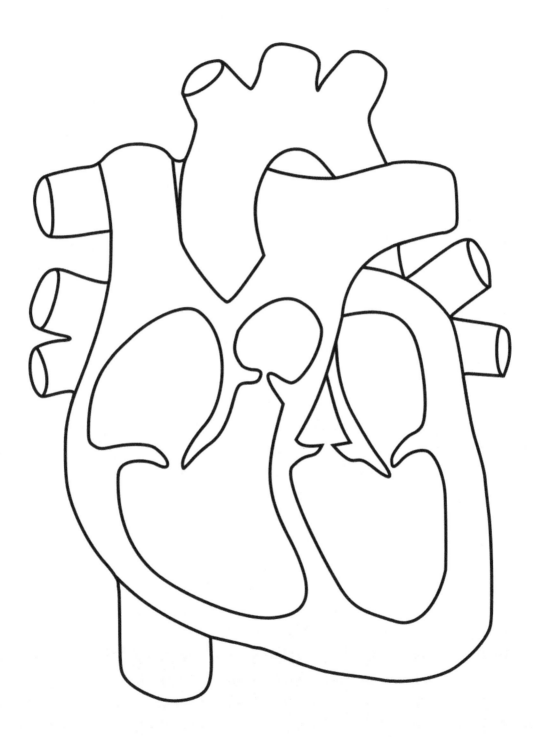

circulatory System

Label the different parts of the circulatory system and answer the questions that follow.

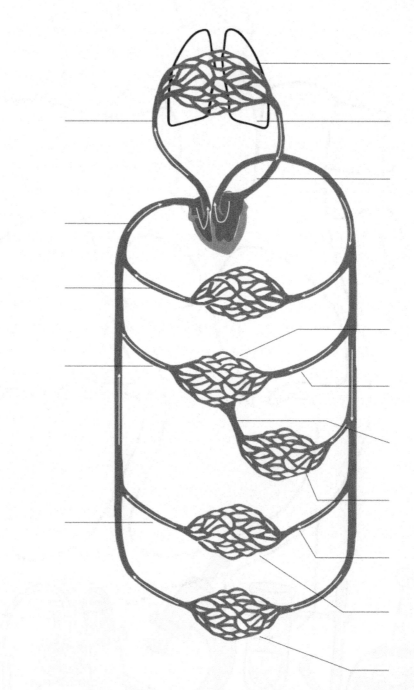

1. How much blood does an average person have?

   _____

2. What color is the oxygen-rich blood?

   _____

3. What color is the oxygen-poor blood?

   _____

4. What is the name of the organ that pumps blood around the body?

   _____

5. How many chambers are there in the human heart?

   _____

6. Name the chambers.

   _____

7. How many blood cells die in the human body in one second?

   _____

8. What prevents blood from flowing backwards in veins?

   _____

9. Name the protein in the red blood cells.

   _____

10. Why is the human circulatory system called the "double circulatory system"?

   _____

   _____

   _____

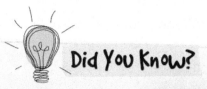
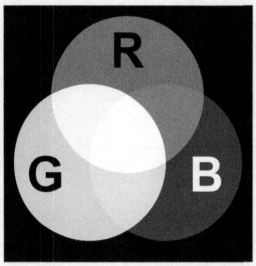

Newton was the first to observe that color is not inherent in an object. The surface of an object reflects some colors and absorbs the rest. We, as viewers, perceive only the reflected colors.

Hence, the color red is not in an apple. The red we see is the wavelength of light that is reflected by the surface of the apple. An object appears white when it reflects all the wavelengths and black when it absorbs them all.

Red, green, and blue are the primary colors on the spectrum. While these three colors combine in a specific ratio to produce white, the ratio can be varied to produce all of the colors in the visible spectrum.

Human eye has two types of cells that detect and respond to different wavelengths of light called rods and cones.

These cells are called photoreceptors as they are sensitive to light. Rods are activated in dim light while cones are stimulated in bright light.

Answers

English Answer Key

Identify the Parts

1. Prepositional phrase

Explanation: The prepositional phrase "of the truck" has a preposition followed by a noun.

2. Verb phrase

Explanation: The verb phrase "had been sleeping" indicates past perfect continuous tense.

3. Verb phrase

Explanation: The verb phrase "will have finished decorating" indicates future perfect continuous tense.

4. Noun phrase

Explanation: The noun phrase "a handmade gift" includes a noun preceded by an article and adjective.

5. Infinitive phrase

Explanation: The infinitive phrase "to take" has the word "to" followed by a verb.

1. with the ponytail

Explanation: This is an adjective prepositional phrase modifying the noun girl. The other phrase in this sentence is "toward the podium" that modifies walking.

2. may take

Explanation: This is a verb phrase in the sentence. The word "avoid" is a verb, but it is not a phrase.

3. one of our neighbors/their stolen car/the investigators

Explanation: These are noun phrases in this sentence. Anyone is acceptable.

4. with great enthusiasm

Explanation: This is an adverb prepositional phrase modifying the verb welcomed.

1. complete

Explanation: The sentence has a complete subject and predicate.

2. incomplete

Explanation: The sentence is incomplete as the first part of comparison (than who?) is missing.

3. complete

Explanation: The sentence has a dependent clause and an independent clause. Stay in the attic is an independent clause where the subject "you" is understood.

4. complete

Explanation: The sentence has two independent clauses.

5. incomplete

Explanation: The sentence is incomplete as the second part of the sentence "what happens when the parents arrive" is missing.

6. incomplete

Explanation: The sentence is incomplete as it does not answer "who identified and documented."

7. complete

Explanation: The sentence has a dependent clause and an independent clause.

8. incomplete

Explanation: The sentence is incomplete as the second part of the sentence "what will happen" is missing.

1. phrase

Explanation: The underlined part is a noun phrase.

2. clause

Explanation: The underlined part is a dependent clause.

3. clause

Explanation: The underlined part is a dependent clause.

4. phrase

Explanation: The underlined part is a noun phrase.

5. clause

Explanation: The underlined part is a dependent clause as it has a subject and a predicate, but cannot stand alone.

6. clause

Explanation: The underlined part is an independent clause.

Sentence Structure

Find the Structure

1. complex sentence
Explanation: The sentence has a dependent clause followed by an independent clause.

2. simple sentence
Explanation: The sentence has an independent clause.

3. complex sentence
Explanation: The sentence has an independent clause followed by a dependent clause.

4. compound–complex sentence
Explanation: Independent clause (We enjoyed the comedy movie), independent clause (we decided to watch it again), and dependent clause (even though it was not what we expected).

5. compound sentence
Explanation: The sentence is composed of two independent clauses.

6. simple sentence
Explanation: The sentence has an introductory phrase followed by an independent clause.

Transform Me

Answers may vary

1. Sam met with an accident; he was unharmed.
Explanation: The two independent clauses can be joined with a semicolon or a comma and conjunction to make a compound sentence.

2. We considered the consequences.
Explanation: Removing the connector "after" and providing a subject will make the clause independent.

3. Since the pizza was cold, we warmed it in the microwave.
Explanation: Adding the word "since" makes the first clause dependent, and a comma is used to connect it with the following independent clause.

4. After the game, the players were tired and needed rest.
Explanation: The two independent clauses are combined with "and" to make a simple sentence.

prepaze

Misplaced and Dangling Modifiers

Is This correct?

1. b. The boy carrying his dog walked toward the door.

Explanation: The other option has the modifier "carrying his dog" misplaced after "door" making it sound as if the door was carrying the dog.

2. a. Leaning against the tree, the farmer's son was hit by a coconut.

Explanation: The other option has the modifier "leaning against the tree" misplaced next to "coconut" making it sound as if the coconut was leaning.

3. b. Working throughout the weekend, they completed the assignment in time.

Explanation: The other option lacks the subject that answers "who completed the assignment?"

Fix Me!

I removed the trash piled up in the corner.

Explanation: The modifier "piled up in the corner" modifies trash, and should be placed next to the word.

The Bunny Club sold almost all the cookies at the bake sale.

Explanation: The modifier "almost" modifies "all," so it should be placed before all. "Almost sold" would imply that they did not sell.

Looking at the sky, she had ideas pouring in.

Explanation: Who had ideas pouring in? Providing the subject "he/she/they/I/" or anything similar is acceptable.

Using the theory of relativity, he explained the behavior of objects.

Explanation: Who explained? Providing the subject "he/she/they/I/" or anything similar is acceptable.

Comma Usage

Add Commas

1. Please welcome the lovely, brilliant, and talented performer.
Explanation: The coordinating adjectives are "lovely, brilliant, and talented."
2. It was a bright, sunny day when we reached Ohio.
Explanation: The coordinating adjectives are "bright, sunny."
3. Her crisp, declamatory, grandiloquent speech left the audience in awe.
Explanation: The coordinating adjectives are "crisp, declamatory, grandiloquent."
4. This dish has Persian, Arabic, and Afghani influences.
Explanation: The coordinating adjectives are "Persian, Arabic, and Afghani."
5. The angry, callous bird pecked at the windows.
Explanation: The coordinating adjectives are "angry, callous."

Which One Is Correct?

1. d) The lion carefully guided her cub across the river, and the photographer captured the precious moment without their knowledge.
Explanation: The comma here joins two independent clauses.
2. c) Pamella bought a car, refrigerator, and washing machine for her parents.
Explanation: The commas here separate items in a series.
3. d) March 14, 2008, is the most important day of my life as I was born on that day.
Explanation: The commas here separate the parenthetical element. When a dependent clause follows an independent clause, a comma is not required to separate the clauses.
4. b) After the test, the children anxiously waited for the results.
Explanation: The comma here provides a pause after the introductory phrase.
5. a) I babysit a couple of lovely, adorable, enthusiastic children on weekends.
Explanation: The commas here separate coordinating adjectives.
6. c) My father, who is a paleontologist, took Stephanie, Irene, Andrew, and me to the museum.
Explanation: The commas here separate the parenthetical element and items in a series.

prepaze

What's My Spelling?

1. a. precursor

2. a. grievous

3. b. disheveled

4. a. feckless

5. b. guileless

Connect Sentences

Words	Correct Spelling
indispensible	indispensable
millennium	✓
accidently	accidentally
consceintious	conscientious
inoculate	✓
flourescent	fluorescent
resucsitation	resuscitation
venaration	veneration
minuscule	✓
allegience	allegiance

Wordiness

Make It Crisp!

1. The lasagna was extremely delicious.
Explanation: Here, the words really and extremely both are used as intensifiers. One of them would suffice.

2. The cities are cleaner than ever before.
Explanation: The phrase "all things considered" can be removed.

3. She took the job to pay her tuition fee.
Explanation: The words "on account

of the fact that it was necessary" were not necessary.

4. The pipelines were connected.
Explanation: The word together is redundant.

5. We came to an agreement that we will share the cottage.
Explanation: The word mutual is redundant.

Context Clues

Use the Context

1. untruthfulness
Explanation: The clue word "truth" and the contradictory word "but" indicate that the underlined word means the opposite of truth.

2. degenerated
Explanation: The clue word "though" suggests contradiction.

3. remind one of something
Explanation: The clue words "memories" indicate reminders from the past.

4. self–centered
Explanation: The definition of the underline word is given in the second part of the sentence, "cannot think or talk about anything other than himself."

5. accommodating
Explanation: The clue words "who take care of all our requests and demands" explains the underlined word.

find the clue

1. claim

Explanation: The clue word "explanation" explains the underlined word.

2. wander aimlessly

Explanation: The clue words "instead of sitting at home" explain the underlined word.

Root Words and Affixes

Match the Meaning

belligerent – hostile

Explanation: bel – is a Latin root that means fight or war.

philanthropy – generosity

Explanation: anthro – is a Greek root that means human or humanity.

heteronym – different

Explanation: hetero – is a Greek root that means different.

inscription – engraving

Explanation: scrib – is a Latin root that means to write.

disrupt – interrupt

Explanation: rupt – is a Latin root that means to break.

Roots	Suffixes	Words	Meaning
mono	chrome	monochrome	a single hue
mono	logue	monologue	a long speech
mono	poly	monotonous	exclusive control of a product or service
mono	phonic	monophonic	one channel of transmission
mono	tony	monotony	one tone
mono	arch	monarch	a ruler
mono	cle	monocle	single eyeglass

Look It Up

1. Ambivalence

Part of speech: noun
Meaning: being uncertain
Sentence: Answer may vary

2. Condone

Part of speech: verb
Meaning: to allow
Sentence: Answer may vary

3. Plausible

Part of speech: adjective
Meaning: reasonable
Sentence: Answer may vary

4. Subordinate

Part of speech: adjective/verb/noun
Meaning: lower rank
Sentence: Answer may vary

5. Ubiquitous

Part of speech: adjective
Meaning: found everywhere
Sentence: Answer may vary

6. Viability

Part of speech: noun
Meaning: ability to work
Sentence: Answer may vary

Spot the odd one

1. Arrive

2. Exactly

3. Flame

4. Scruffy

5. Kind

Identify the Allusion

1. greedy and unkind

Explanation: This is a literary allusion referring to the character Scrooge from Charles Dickens' novel, A Christmas Carol.

2. impossible situation

Explanation: This is a biblical allusion referring to Jesus comparing the chances of a rich man entering the kingdom of God with the camel getting through the eye of a needle.

3. someone who cannot be conquered

Explanation: This is a mythological allusion referring to the Greek goddess Nemesis. A nemesis is a challenge or opponent who a person cannot defeat.

4. genius

Explanation: This is a historical allusion referring to Albert Einstein: one of the greatest scientists and intellect.

5. vigilant

Explanation: This is a mythological allusion referring to the Greek legend Argus who had 100 eyes.

Find the Allusion

1. Gordian knot

Explanation: This is a mythological allusion referring to King Gordius who tied a wagon to a column with a complex knot that only Alexander the Great was able to cut through. A Gordian knot is a complex problem, and to cut the Gordian knot is to resolve the problem.

2. Romeo

Explanation: This is a literary allusion referring to the character Romeo from Shakespeare's popular play. This allusion shows that someone is passionate and expresses himself/herself explicitly.

3. Garden of Eden

Explanation: This is a biblical allusion referring to the "garden of God" that is used to describe something as a paradise.

4. Herculean

Explanation: This is a mythological allusion referring to the Greek hero Hercules. A Herculean task is very hard to perform and requires great strength.

5. Judas

Explanation: This is a biblical allusion. Judas Iscariot was one of the twelve original apostles of Jesus Christ. He is known for his betrayal of Jesus in exchange for thirty pieces of silver. Judas is a classic example of betrayal.

Make Allusions

Answers will vary

Word Analogy

Connect the Analogies

1. waitress : restaurant :: lawyer : courtroom
Explanation: Functional relationship: a waitress works in a restaurant as a lawyer works in a courtroom.

2. pebble : boulder :: pond: sea
Explanation: Degree relationship: pebble is a small boulder or rock as the pond is a smaller unit of a sea.

3. anaconda : snake :: mahogany : timber
Explanation: Type relationship: anaconda is a type of a snake as mahogany is a type of timber.

4. gallant : valiant :: docile : compliant
Explanation: Synonyms: gallant is a synonym of valiant as docile is a synonym of compliant.

5. troupe : dancers :: shoal : fish
Explanation: Collective noun: a group of dancers is called a troupe as a large number of fish is called a shoal.

6. polite : rude :: awkward : relaxed
Explanation: Antonyms: polite is the opposite of rude as awkward is the opposite of relaxed.

Find the Matching Pair

1. b

Explanation: Hierarchy relationship. A nurse assists a doctor as a secretary assists a businessman.

2. b

Explanation: Quantity and unit relationship. Pressure is measured in Pascal as temperature is measured in degree Farenheit.

3. c

Explanation: Worker and product relationship. Choreographer choreographs Tango as a dramatist writes plays.

4. c

Explanation: Things and keeping place relationship. Medicines are kept in dispensary as bees are kept in apiary

5. a

Explanation: Animal and young one relationship. Young one of a cockroach is nymph as young one of a swan is cygnet

Write Analogy

Answer may vary

1. sample answer – paper : book

Explanation: The relationship is – raw material : product.

2. sample answer – teacher : school

Explanation: The relationship is – worker : workplace.

3. sample answer – tennis : court

Explanation: The relationship is – game : playing area.

Riddle

Answer: BXT

Explanation: In the first pair, the first set of letters is counted backward with intervals of 5 and the second set is counted backward with intervals of 3. The second set begins with the same letter with which the first set ends. The second pair follows the same logic.

Synonyms and Antonyms

Spot the odd one

1. introvert	3. indigenous	5. embezzle	7. permeate
2. endeavor	4. accolade	6. vigorous	8. garrulous

Find the Match

1. mischievous – playful	3. create – develop	5. ruin – waste	7. accurate – correct
2. answer – respond	4. hurry – rush	6. drop – descend	8. cold – chilly

feasible – impracticable	erratic – predictable
astute – witless	cognizance – ignorance
disheveled – orderly	exasperate – appease

1. plan – design   3. expend – spend   5. obtain – acquire

2. wreck – shatter   4. expose – reveal   6. silent – quiet

Connotation and Denotation

Complete Me

1. economical

Explanation: Economical has a positive connotation, while stingy has a negative connotation.

2. easygoing

Explanation: Easygoing has a positive connotation, while indifferent has a negative connotation.

3. inquisitive

Explanation: Inquisitive has a positive connotation, while prying has a negative connotation.

1. scrutinizing other's work

Explanation: Scrutinizing has a negative connotation, while studying has a positive connotation.

2. exploits

Explanation: The word exploits has a negative connotation, while uses has a neutral connotation.

3. wilful

Explanation: The word wilful has a negative connotation, while resolute has a positive connotation.

Neutral, Positive, or Negative?

1. Neutral: secure; positive: confident; negative: egotistical

2. Neutral: conversational; positive: chatty; negative: jabbering

The Emperor's New Suit

Story Elements

1. c) He is often found in the dressing–room trying on new clothes

2. b) Vain

3. b) Obsequious

4. c) They appeared to work hard at the empty looms.

5. a) The emperor knew from the beginning that he was tricked by the swindlers.

6. c) Humourous

7. c) They follow something that they know is absurd just because people around them believe it is the right thing to do.

8. b) We should not blindly follow fashion trends or follow a crowd without knowing the facts.

9. b) Pride and vanity

10. c) He was too proud to accept his gullibility.

Idioms

1. all the way

2. to deceive someone

3. very similar

Decode the Word

		E	M	P	E	R	O	R	
			W	E	A	V	E	R	
	C	O	U	R	T	I	E	R	
M	I	N	I	S	T	E	R		
		S	O	L	D	I	E	R	
C	H	A	M	B	E	R	L	A	I	N

| M | E | T | T | L | E |

Poem Appreciation

1. b
Explanation: The eleventh line of the poem shows when the neighbors mend their walls.

2. c
Explanation: The neighbor comes across as stubborn and unwilling to change. A traditionalist is a person who adheres to traditional views.

3. c
Explanation: Line 12 shows how the author lets the neighbor beyond the hill know it is time to mend the walls.

4. b
Explanation: Throughout the poem (for example: lines 1 and 23), the author hints that the wall has no purpose.

5. c
Explanation: Fence symbolises the gap between people. Some people think it is important for a healthy relationship and privacy while some think of the gap as a barrier between two people.

6. a
Explanation: This poem is written in blank verse comprising iambic pentameter. The choice free verse is incorrect as it means a poem written with no rhyme or meter.

7. a
Explanation: The use of the pronouns I and my suggest that the poem is written in first person: from the point of view of the author.

8. b
Explanation: The author questions the neighbor's unwillingness to change and says the neighbor follows traditional ways, but he himself builds the wall every year, which is a tradition.

9. c
Explanation: Lines repeated at the same interval is called as refrain. The line "Good fences make good neighbours" is repeated in the poem.

10. c
Explanation: This poem is about the author's claim to openness to change and know his neighbor versus the neighbor's repressive nature toward change.

Poem Analysis

Answer may vary

1. **Explanation:** The author says the walls are unnecessary and contradicts this point of view with the neighbor's view, which is to retain the wall to maintain good neighbors.

2. **Explanation:** *I see him there / Bringing a stone grasped firmly by the top / In each hand, like an old–stone savage armed.*

In this simile, the speaker compares his neighbor to a stone–age savage indirectly suggesting his thoughts to being traditional.

3. **Explanation:** The title is significant as it has two meanings, one literal and the other figurative. The wall symbolises the gap between the two neighbors. The author wonders how the neighbor lacks curiosity and assumes it is because of his traditional mindset. However, the neighbors evidently come together only during the mending wall season, and the author compares it to a sport.

Crossword Puzzle

Across

2. closure – gap

3. obedience – mischief

6. damage – mend

7. laugh – yelp

Down

1. civilized – savage

4. prey – hunter

5. thawed – froze

Story Analysis

1. b

Explanation: The cat informed the animals.

2. c

Explanation: The ass was not gullible or optimistic as it did not believe the cat. The ass is a skeptic as it asks for proof and refuses to believe.

3. c

Explanation: The elephant sent the ass to check the authenticity of the picture.

4. b

Explanation: Each animal saw its own reflection by standing between the mirror and the picture.

5. b

Explanation: The most certain thing that would follow is that the animals would be ignorant of the truth. The animals spreading the rumor is possible, but it is not the most certain choice here.

6. a

Explanation: It is true that the picture is flat. The bear says the cat and ass have lied, but it is not logically true. They said whatever they saw.

7. c

Explanation: The story is written from a third person point of view. The narrator is not a part of the story.

8. a

Explanation: The story revolves around how the perspectives of each of the characters differ. The story is also about the power of knowledge, demonstrating how some accept what is told to them and some seek evidence before accepting what is told to them.

9. a

Explanation: The other animals failed to see the picture, whereas the cat appreciated the beauty of the picture as it was able to see it without standing between the mirror and the picture. The ass was smart enough to seek evidence, but it failed to see the picture.

10. c

Explanation: The leader of the animals, the elephant, and the other animals were ready to accept the picture to be as admirable as described by the cat, but the ass made them verify it (though it was true). Similarly, the media may feed us any news, which we should not believe without evidence.

artist – innovative

Explanation: The picture that can be admired using a mirror shows the artist was innovative and brilliant.

housecat – intelligent

Explanation: The cat is intelligent as it knew how to admire the picture without standing between the mirror and the picture.

ass – suspicious

Explanation: The ass was suspicious of the picture.

elephant – gullible

Explanation: The elephant is gullible as it believed when the cat said the picture was wonderful, and the elephant believed the other animals when they said the cat was a liar.

cow – ignorant

Explanation: The cow is ignorant and follows whatever the leader (elephant) says.

Sequencing

1. HOUSECAT
2. BEAR
3. COW
4. TIGER

5. LION
6. LEOPARD
7. CAMEL
8. ELEPHANT

Word Building

ETHEREAL	REVIVAL	EVIDENCE	UNAPPEASABLE
SESQUIPEDALIAN	ASSAILED	WITNESS	
SUSPICION	PERCEPTIBLE	WROTH	

Beautiful Harbor of Sitka

Understanding Text

1. holiday
Explanation: The answer holiday is in the opening statement.
2. both of the above
Explanation: The last sentence of the first paragraph holds the answer.
3. People of different races live in Sitka.
Explanation: The statement about people of different races is true. According to the second paragraph, the other two statements are untrue.
4. the mariner
Explanation: As far out as the eye can reach the beautiful isles
break the cold sea into bewitching inlets and lure the mariner to shelter from evil outside waves.
5. lush vegetation
Explanation: Verdure means lush vegetation. The village is surrounded by lush vegetation. Mountains are on both sides.

6. Russian governor
Explanation: The author describes the large square house that once housed the Russian governor.
7. The governor's house is no longer feasible for accommodation.
Explanation: The author says the building is no longer feasible for anyone to live, and it will be only remembered by the people of the town.
8. architectural buildings
Explanation: The concluding statement holds the answer.
9. first person
Explanation: The use of the pronoun "our" indicates the text is in first person.
10. to describe the town
Explanation: The author uses ample descriptions to help the readers visualize the town.

Word Building

Sentences may vary.

1. compound sentence

Explanation: The sentence consists of two independent clauses.

2. simple sentence

Explanation: The sentence consists of an independent clause followed by a phrase.

3. simple sentence

Explanation: The sentence consists of an independent clause followed by a series of phrases.

4. complex sentence

Explanation: The sentence consists of a dependent clause followed by an independent clause.

5. compound sentence

Explanation: The sentence consists of three independent clauses.

Data Interpretation

1. 273 million
2. Bangladesh
3. Ethiopia
4. United States
5. Pakistan
6. Nigeria
7. Russia
8. Ethiopia – United States
9. Mexico – Brazil – Indonesia
10. Japan

Flag Quiz

1. Nigeria
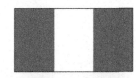

2. Bangladesh

3. Japan

4. Ethiopia

5. United States

6. Pakistan

7. Russia

8. Mexico

9. Brazil

10. Indonesia

Country	Nationality
Nigeria	Nigerian
Bangladesh	Bangladeshi
Japan	Japanese
Ethiopia	Ethiopian
United States	American
Pakistan	Pakistani
Russia	Russian
Mexico	Mexican
Brazil	Brazilian
Indonesia	Indonesian

Math Answer Key

Ratio

a. Ratio – 6:4; Fraction – $\dfrac{3}{2}$; Simplest form – 3:2

b. Ratio – 4:3; Fraction – $\dfrac{4}{3}$; Simplest form – 4:3

c. Ratio – 5:5; Fraction – $\dfrac{5}{5}$; Simplest form – 1:1

Percentage Representation

a. $\dfrac{2}{5}$, 40%

b. $\dfrac{3}{8}$, 37.5%

c. $\dfrac{5}{4}$, 125%

Unit Rate

a. 280:5, thus each teacher will manage 56 students.

b. $\dfrac{1}{8}$ th of 40 is 5. So each child gets 5 chocolates. There are 40 chocolates thus, there are 8 children.

c. $\dfrac{10}{9}$ miles per hour

a. Oranges : A pack of 6 oranges @$4

b. Eggs : A pack of 3 eggs @$1.50

c. Milk : 2 gallon of milk @$1.80

d. Pens : A pack of 10 pens @$6

Ratio of Girls to Boys

1:3; 1 ; 3 boys and a girl; totally 10 teams

2 more vehicles

a. 2:3

b. 3:4

c. $\frac{3}{5} : \frac{8}{13}$ (or) 60% : 61.5%

Proportional Relationships

Which Variety Would Cost Less?

Washington red variety and green apple variety are least priced @$1.30 per lb

The measurement would be 20 inches * 50 inches.

True or False

a. True

b. False

c. True

d. False

e. False

a. $x = \frac{12}{5}$

b. $e = \frac{7}{5}$

c. $x = \frac{3}{2}$

d. $y = 27$

Equation of Proportionality

a. 30 gms/granola

b. $y = \frac{x}{30}$

c. y intercept is y value when x=0. Thus intercept is 0. So, there are zero bars when the weight is zero.

Slope is the change in y for unit change in x which is also unit rate. Thus, the slope is $\frac{1}{30}$. So, $\frac{1}{30}$ of the bar weighs 1 gram.

Simple Interest

b. The unit rate is $200/year.

c. $y = 200x$

a.

Period (x)	Accumulated interest (y)
1	200
2	400
3	600
4	800
5	1000

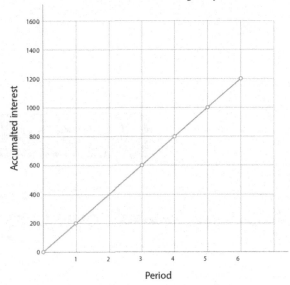

Accumlated interest for a given period

d. y is 200 times x

The Tax Problem

a. The unit rate is 6% .

c. $y = 0.06x + 1$

b.

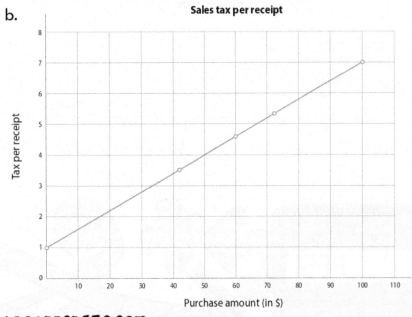

Sales tax per receipt

a. ratio of immune to diseased = 280:120 = 7:3

b. percentage of vulnerable population = 120/400*100% = 30%

a. The circle has one portion shaded in gray and the other portion shaded in white. So it can be represented by $\dfrac{1}{2}$.

b. The circle has one portion shaded in gray out of four portions of the circle. So it is represented as $\dfrac{1}{4}$.

c. The circle has one portion shaded in gray out of three portions of the circle. So it is represented as $\dfrac{1}{3}$.

d. $\dfrac{1}{2} + \dfrac{1}{4} + \dfrac{1}{3}$, LCM of 2,4 and 3 is 12. So, $\dfrac{6}{12} + \dfrac{3}{12} + \dfrac{4}{12} = \dfrac{13}{12}$.

Classify the Numbers

a. integer = −4

rational = $\dfrac{1}{2}$, 2.3, $-\dfrac{3}{5}$

b. whole = 0, 6

integer = −8, 0, 6

rational = $-\dfrac{3}{5}$; $\dfrac{1}{3}$

c. whole = 32, $\sqrt{49}$

integer = −56, 32, $\sqrt{49}$

rational = 0.45, $-\dfrac{12}{19}$

Number	Absolute value	Opposite value
a. $-\dfrac{12}{17}$	$\dfrac{12}{17}$	$\dfrac{12}{17}$
b. 1.34	1.34	−1.34
c. $-\sqrt{4}$	$\sqrt{4}$	$\sqrt{4}$

Locate on Number Line

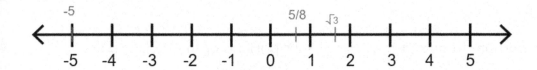

Operations on Rational Numbers

a. $-4 + 2 = -2$

b. $3 + (-2) = 1$

c. $7 - (-1) = 8$

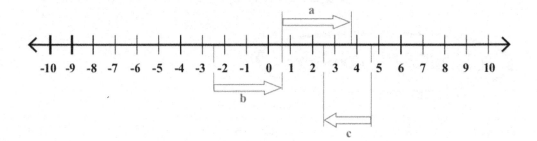

a. $\dfrac{1}{2} + 3\dfrac{1}{4} = 3\dfrac{3}{4}$

b. $-2.3 + 3 = 0.7$

c. $4.8 - 2.3 = 2.5$

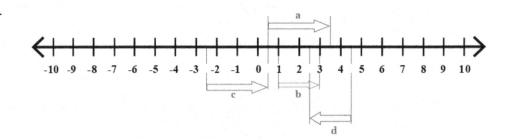

a. -2

b. $\dfrac{334}{99}$ (or) 3.374

c. $\dfrac{81}{14}$ (or) 5.786

Conversions

a. $\dfrac{13}{5}$ b. $\dfrac{89}{7}$ c. $\dfrac{227}{20}$

a. 30.625

b. 15.429

c. 21.857

prepaze

How Much Does Sam Save?

He would save $260.

Since each row has to be equal

$\frac{4}{8} = \frac{1}{2}$ in the first row.

$\frac{6}{12} = \frac{1}{2}$ in the second row.

$\frac{7}{14} = \frac{1}{2}$ in the third row.

$\frac{1}{8}$	$\frac{2}{8}$	$\frac{1}{8}$
$\frac{1}{12}$	$\frac{3}{12}$	$\frac{2}{12}$
$\frac{1}{14}$	$\frac{2}{14}$	$\frac{4}{14}$

Temperature Math

The temperature on Tuesday is 26 degrees.

a. Lisa takes 3 hrs

b. Allen takes 1.5 hrs. John takes 2 hrs. Thus out of the three, Allen takes the least time.

c. Allen, John, Lisa

An Eggey Problem

a. 9.6 g pepper powder

b. 0.6 g per egg

a. $x = \frac{4}{3}$

b. $z = \frac{4}{5}$

b. $7x + 14$

c. $5x + 3y + 5x - 5y = 10x - 2y$

d. $7v - 2 + 4v - 7 = 11v - 9$

Expression in Standard form

a. $4a - 30b + 40c$

a. $3a$; $3 \times (-2) = -6$

d. $-5x$; $-5 \times \dfrac{1}{5} = -1$

b. $16a - 14b + 21c$

b. $7b$; $7 \times (-1) = -7$

e. $10y$; $10 \times (-\dfrac{1}{10}) = -1$

c. $-30a + 9b - 18c$

c. $8c$; $8 \times 3 = 24$

Who Is Right?

Anna is right, because she correctly added the variables together and correctly applied any order (the commutative property), changing the order of addition

Samuel is wrong, because he swapped the coefficients.

a. $-12m + 6 + 3m - 11 = -9m - 5$

b. $5g - 8 - 9g = -4g - 8$

c. $-8x - 9 - (-5x + 2) = -3x - 11$

Represent as Expressions

a. Expression 1: m - 0.15m

Expression 2: 0.85m

b. ¼ n

c. Expression 1: d + 0.06d

Expression 2: 1.06d

d. 10y + 5

e. Let the cost of the bill be x.

Expression 1: x + 0.12x

Expression 2: 1.12x

Simplify the Expressions

a. −13g − 3

b. 3h + 25

c. 7j + 7k

d. 6 + 26a

e. −6m + 37n

a. 24 + 4x

b. 5a

c. 28x

d. 4x + 4

e. 16p

Solve the Problems

a. Perimeter of the park = 10x

b. Perimeter of the backyard garden = 18x

c. x + 7

5(m + 5n)

Five people each buy a ticket and five packets of bird feed, so the cost is five times the quantity of a ticket and five packets of bird feed.

5m + 25n

There are five tickets and 25 packets of bird feed in total. The total cost will be five times the cost of the tickets, plus 25 times the cost of the packets of bird feed.

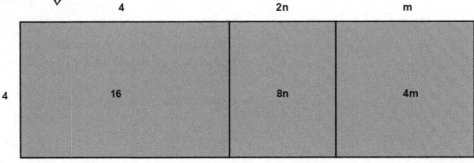

b. 16 + 8n + 4m

c. Area of a rectangle = length x breadth = 4 (4 + 2n + m)

$$= 16 + 8n + 4m$$

a. 9x

b. (1 - 63y)/7

c. m + 5

d. a - 5

e. -3x + 9

a. $\dfrac{12k}{5}$

b. 1 inch = $\dfrac{1}{12}$ feet

$\dfrac{5y}{6}$ inches = $\dfrac{5y}{72}$ feet

c. 1 oz = $\dfrac{1}{16}$ pounds

6x oz = $\dfrac{6x}{16}$ = $\dfrac{3x}{8}$ pounds

d. 1 g = $\dfrac{1}{1000}$ kg

5x g = $\dfrac{5x}{1000}$ = $\dfrac{x}{200}$ kg

e. s = 2x miles/hr

Distributive Property

a. 14y - 7

b. 5a/9 - 1/7

c. (19b - 2)/15

d. (25p - 18)/24

e. (5x + 2)/12

Find the Errors

Problems with incorrect solutions	What is the mistake?	Correct solution with steps
$5x + 2(4x) - 7$ Step 1: $5x + 8x - 7$ Step 2: $6x$	7 was subtracted from the sum of 5x and 8x	$5x + 2(4x) - 7$ Step 1: $5x + 8x - 7$ Step 2: $13x - 7$
$12 - 4(7 - y)$ Step 1: $8(7 - y)$ Step 2: $56 - 8y$	4 was subtracted from 12 which is incorrect. Distributive property should have been used to distribute the terms $4(7 - y)$ in the first step.	$12 - 4(7 - y)$ Step 1: $12 - 28 + 4y$ Step 2: $-16 + 4y$
$11v - 2(-2v + 5)$ Step 1: $11v + 4v + 10$ Step 2: $15v + 10$	While using the distributive property the second sign is not changed.	$11v - 2(-2v + 5)$ Step 1: $11v + 4v - 10$ Step 2: $15v - 10$

prepaze

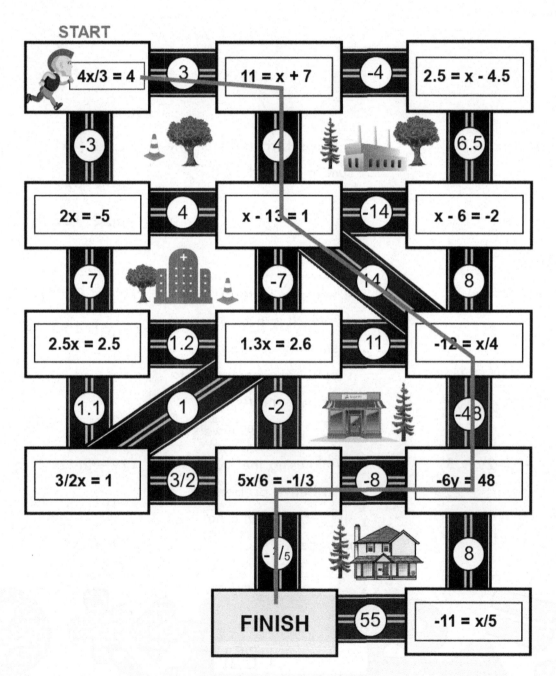

START

| 4x/3 = 4 | 3 | 11 = x + 7 | -4 | 2.5 = x - 4.5 |

-3   4   6.5

| 2x = -5 | 4 | x - 13 = 1 | -14 | x - 6 = -2 |

-7   -7   14   8

| 2.5x = 2.5 | 1.2 | 1.3x = 2.6 | 11 | -12 = x/4 |

1.1   1   -2   -48

| 3/2x = 1 | 3/2 | 5x/6 = -1/3 | -8 | -6y = 48 |

-2/5   8

| FINISH | 55 | -11 = x/5 |

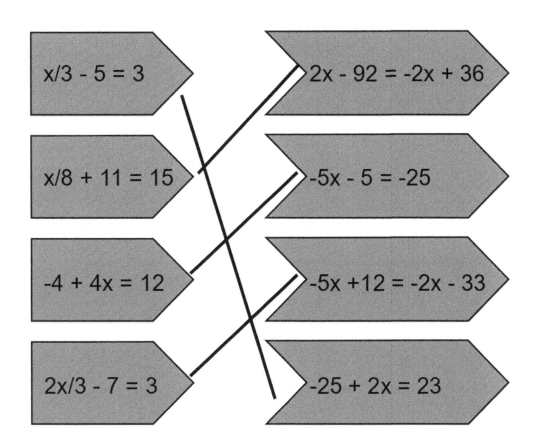

a. x= 12 is not a solution.

b. x= $-4\frac{1}{3}$ is not a solution.

c. x= 50 is not a solution.

d. x= $-1\frac{1}{5}$ is not a solution.

e. x= 40 is a solution.

a. length = 10.5 inches, width = 3.5 inches

b. One number is 35 and the other number is 37

c. Jack has $10.40 and Fardin has $5.15.

d. Jackson's age is 32 years and Ronaldo's age is 25 years.

	Present age	Within five years	
Jackson's age	x	x+ 5	} Total is 67
Ronaldo's age	x- 7	x- 7+ 5	

e. The numbers are 36 and 54.

Solve the Inequalities

b.   x > 1

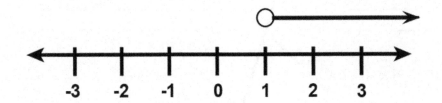

c.   x ≥ -4

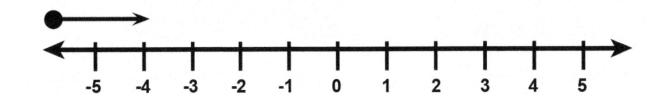

d.   x > 2

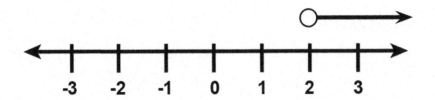

e.   x ≤ 3

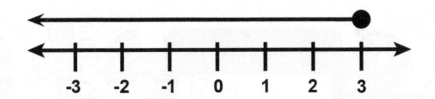

prepaze

a. $1050

b. Equation → $32 + 3x = 80$

Cost of each scarf is $16.

c. Equation → $60 + 48 + 2x = 150$

Cost of wooden antiques = $60

Cost of carpet = $ 48

Cost of two chairs = $42

So, cost of each chair = $42 ÷ 2 = $21

d. Equation: $25 + 15 + 10x = 90$

$x = 5$

Cost of one cap is $5

b. $x > 2$

c. $x \geq 1$

d. $x < -2$

e. $x \leq -1$

Describe the Banner Length

a. $2 (20 + w) \leq 48$

b.

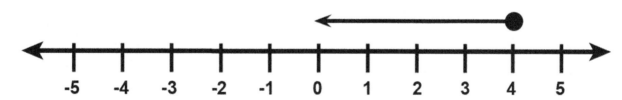

c. $w = 4$ or $w < 4$

Equation → $15000(1 - \dfrac{n}{5}) = 6000$

$n = 3$

After 3 years he should plan to replace the car in order to receive this trade-in value.

Lucas Weekend Drive

	Rate (mph)	Time (hours)	Distance (miles)
Lucas speed 1	18	t	18t
Lucas speed 2	21	5 - t	21(5 - t)

Equation → 18t + 21(5 - t) = 90; t = 5

So, Lucas rode at 18mph for 5 hours.

a. Cost of trousers = 59.88 - 2(15.14)

= $29.60

b. Expression → 2y + 29.60

c. Equation → 2y + 29.60 = 59.88

d. Cost of one shirt is $15.14

a. My number is 2.

b. The number is -2.

c. The number is 1.

Let y represent the number of nights

$40y + 140 \leq 500$; $y \leq 9$

Myra can afford up to 9 nights

Let the cost of printing one coffee mug be $t and cost of printing one t-shirt be $(t + 0.15) Equation → $30(t + t + 0.15) = 139.50$

$t = 2.25$

So, cost of printing one coffee mug is $2.25

and cost of printing one t-shirt is $(2.25 + 0.15) = $2.40

Let x be the number of minutes.

1st plan $= 0.24x$

2nd plan $= 32.39 + 0.06x$

Equation → $0.24x > 32.39 + 0.06x$

$x > 179.94 \approx 180$ minutes

James should use the phone for more than 180 mins

Scale Drawings

a. Scale factor $= \dfrac{3}{5}$

b.

	Quotient of corresponding horizontal distances	Quotient of corresponding vertical distances	Scale factor as a percentage
Drawings 2 to 1	1.6	1.6	160%

c. Shape 2 to shape 1 is an enlargement. The scale factor is $166\dfrac{2}{3}$ %

d. The scale factor from shape 1 to shape 3 is 15%. Examples for verification may vary.

e. Scale factor $= \dfrac{5}{4}$

a.

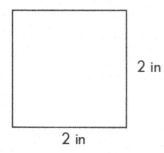

2 in

2 in

b.

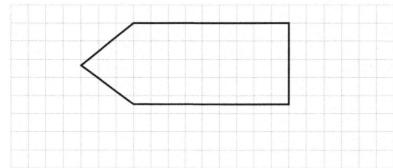

The scale drawing is an enlargement.

c. Olivia's garden is 7.2 ft long and 6.25 ft wide.

7.2 cm

6.25 cm

prepaze

a. The actual length of the wing span is 92 ft

b. Her mural will be 5 ft long on the wall.

c. Part A - The scale factor is $166\frac{2}{3}$%

Part B - The dimensions of the large postcard is 15 inches by 20 inches

Part C - The area of the medium-sized postcard is $44\frac{4}{9}$ % of the larger postcard

a. scale factor of big to small $= \dfrac{5}{3}$

area of big pizza to small pizza $= \dfrac{100}{36} = \dfrac{25}{9} = (\dfrac{5}{3})^2$

The area of the free space in the smaller box is 7.74 in^2

b. The actual area of the store is 675 ft^2

Unknown Angles

Vertical angles	<AEC and <BED, <CEB and <DEA
Adjacent angles	Examples: <AEC and <CEF; <BED and <DEG
Angles on a line	Example: <AEC, <CEF and <FEB <AEC, <AEG and <GED
Angles at a point	<AEC, <CEF, <FEB, <BED, <DEG, <GEA

prepaze

Angle Measures

a. $x = 30°$

b. $m = 47$ $n = 52$

c. The measurement of $\angle AOB = 73°$

The measurement of $\angle BOC = 107°$

d. $x = 36$ and $y = 24$

Angle Fun

a. Drawing will vary. The angles must measure $36°$ and $144°$

b.

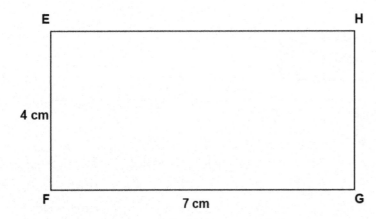

c.

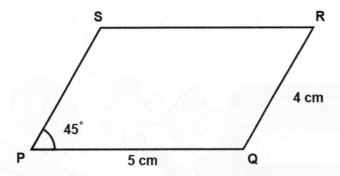

prepaze

c. Altitude to PQ - 2.8 cm
Altitude to QR - 3.5 cm

d.

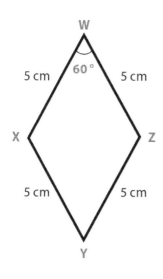

e.

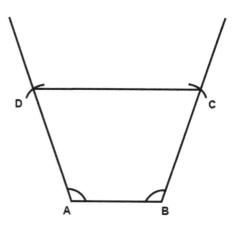

f. Answers will vary.

Constructing Triangles

a. Drawings will vary.

The three angles in a triangle must add to $180°$. Since the two angle measures add up to more than $180°$, such a triangle does not exist.

b.

Triangles	Identical/non-identical/ not necessarily identical.	Justification
 O M ⬜ ⬜ N P	Identical	The triangles are identical by two sides and non-included $90°$ (or greater) angle condition. The corresponding triangles MPO and NPO matches two pairs of equal sides and one pair of equal angles.

	Not necessarily identical	The triangles are not necessarily identical by the two angles and side opposite a given angle condition. In triangle ABC the marked side is adjacent to the angle marked with a single arc mark. In triangle WXY, the marked side is not adjacent to the angle marked with a single arc mark.
	Not identical	The triangles are not identical since a correspondence that matches the two marked equal pairs of sides also matches sides VX and XY, which are not equal in length.

The Bridge Problem

Yes, M is the midpoint of BC. The triangles are identical by the two sides and included angle condition. The correspondence △ABM ⟷ △DCM matches two pairs of equal sides and one pair of included equal angles. Since the triangles are identical, we can use the correspondence to conclude that BM = CM, which makes M the midpoint, by definition.

Slicing Solids

Slice as a 2D Shape

i.

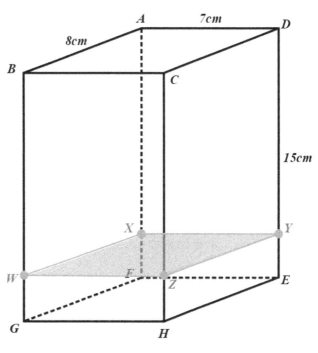

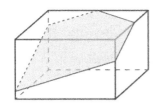

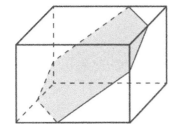

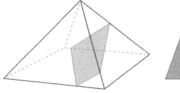

ii. Sides WZ and XY are 7 cm in length. Sides WX and ZY are 8 cm in length.

iii. Slice WXYZ is parallel to faces ABCD and EFGH and perpendicular to faces CDEH, ADEF, ABGF and BCHG.

12.

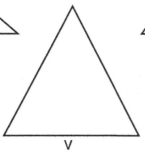

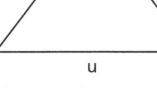

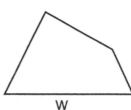

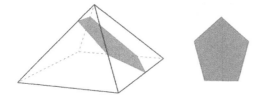

Circle Problems

a. We can find - radius, area and circumference using the diameter.

$R = \dfrac{d}{2}$;　area $= \pi \left(\dfrac{d}{2}\right)^2$; circumference $= 2\pi \left(\dfrac{d}{2}\right)$

b. The area of the ring is 175.84 cm^2 (π taken as 3.14)

c. The area of the windows is the sum of the areas of the two quarter circles and the two squares. If the span of windows is 12 feet across the bottom, then each window is 3 feet wide on the bottom. The radius of the quarter circles is 3 feet, so the area for one quarter circle window is $A = \dfrac{1}{4}\pi \,(3\ ft)^2$, or $A \approx 7.065\ ft^2$. The area of one square window is $A = (3\ ft)^2$, or $9\ ft^2$.

The total area is A = 2 (area of quarter circles) + 2 (area of squares)

$$A \approx 2\,(7.065\ ft^2\,) + 2(9ft^2)$$

$$A \approx 32.13\ ft^2$$

d. The area of the circle with the diameter of 10 m has a radius of 5 m.

The area of this circle is $A = \pi\,(5\ m^2)$ or $25\ \pi\ m^2$

The area of the circle with the diameter of 20 m has a radius of 10 m.

The area of this circle is $A = \pi\,(10\ m^2)$ or $100\ \pi\ m^2$

The ratio of the diameters is 20 to 10 that is 2:1. Whereas, the ratio of the areas is 100 to 25 that is 4:1

The Role of Circumference

a. Perimeter = 22.28 cm

b. A $\approx$ 9.8 m^2

c. C = 12π cm

prepaze

a. The area is approximately 81.12 cm^2

b. The area is approximately 157 cm^2

c. The area is 301.5 cm^2

a. The tank can hold 960 ft^3 of water.

b. To fill the tank, 7180 gallons of water is needed

c. The water level dropped by approximately 1 foot.

d. The surface area that needs to be covered is 656 ft^2

a. The surface area of the figure is 410 m^2

b. The surface area of the prism is $226\frac{11}{20}$ cm^2

c. The surface area is 6 cm^2

d. The surface area of the solid is $10\frac{1}{2}$ in^2

a. The volume of the solid is $53\frac{3}{5}$ cm^3

b. The volume of the prism is $\frac{1}{4}$ in^3

a. The area of the counter space is $\approx$ 13.1 ft^2

b. The paper will wrap 57 cans.

c. The surface area of the box is 656 cm^2

a. $(x + 1)(x + 2) = x^2 + 2x + x + 2$

$\qquad = x^2 + 3x + 2$

	x	2
x	x^2	2x
1	x	2

b. $(x + 3)(x + 4) = x^2 + 3x + 4x + 12$

$\qquad = x^2 + 7x + 12$

	x	3
x	x^2	3x
4	4x	12

c. $(x - 3)(x + 3) = x^2 - 3x + 3x - 9$

$\qquad = x^2 - 9$

	x	3
x	x^2	3x
− 3	− 3x	− 9

d. Substitute $x = 5$ in part (c)

$(5 - 3)(5 + 3) = 5^2 - 9$

$\qquad = 25 - 9$

$\qquad = 16$

prepaze

Random Sampling

a. $\dfrac{8}{44} \cong 0.18$

b. $(2+5+10)/44 = \dfrac{17}{44} \cong 0.39$

c.

Number of Electronics Used	1	2	3	4	5	6	7
Probability	0.045	0.114	0.227	0.341	0.182	0.068	0.023

Biased or Unbiased

a. Biased, because it is subjective to people living in just one of the states.
b. Unbiased. Each customer is likely to be interviewed as the other.
c. Biased. Other grade students were not considered.
d. Unbiased. The population is random.

a. He could have interviewed some of the girls too.
Instead of checking their lunchboxes, he could have asked for their favorite lunch.
He could have included the whole class in the survey.

b. He could have checked the papers randomly.
He could have included the papers of the students who did not do well in the test.
He could have increased the size of his sample.

a. Interview students from different primary schools.
b. 56% of all the boys in the Basketball team like Reading.

a. ≅1054 students

b. ≅558 cupcakes

Flight 1 ≅ 24,

Flight 2 ≅ 21,

Flight 3 ≅ 17,

Flight 4 ≅ 38

a. 304 red-tailed parrots

b. 875 monkeys

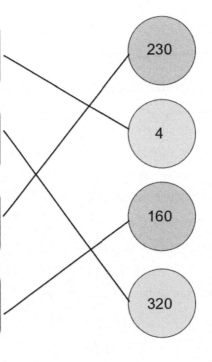

Predict Who Will Win?

a. The sample of 50 should be such that each student has a fair chance of being selected. The randomness can be ensured by numbering the students and selecting 50 distinct numbers.

b. $\dfrac{23}{50} \cong 0.46$. 0.46 is less than 0.5(50%). So it is not a good estimate to predict that Toby will win the election.

a. 63.1

b. No, the sample mean will vary according to the sample values.

c. Yes. 62.92

The reading time is 3.3 hours (or) 3 hrs 18 mins.

Mary's Average Score

82 marks

a. Mean age = 23

b. Only one employee, Peter.

c. Older than mean = Bright, Mark, George, Pinto Younger than mean = Micheal, Allen, Chris

d. Median age = 23.5

Peter's Average Goalscore

a. Average is 3 goals per game

b. Median = 3. In 2 games the goals exceeded the median number.

c. Most common number of goals = 3

a. Average price/toy = $3.20

b. Mode = 5 and 1

c. Median =2.5, 5 toys priced above median

Alice and Holly

a. Average distance of Alice = 3.95 miles Average distance of Holly = 3.73 miles, Alice covers more distance.

b. MAD of Alice=0.47 MAD of Holly= 0.43

c. Deviation is more for Alice.

a. Average cost in developed country=$19.8 ; average cost in developing country=$17.6

b. MAD developed=0.72 MAD developing=2.08

Sharp variation in prices in developing countries, thus pricing is more stable in developed countries.

prepaze

Probability Models

Spinning Wheel Problem

a. $\dfrac{3}{8}$

b. $\dfrac{6}{8}$

c. $\dfrac{5}{8}$

d. $\dfrac{1}{4}$

a. $\dfrac{1}{2}$

b. $\dfrac{3}{4}$

c. $\dfrac{3}{4}$

a. $\dfrac{1}{5}$

b. $\dfrac{3}{10}$

c. picking a blue marble

d. picking a green marble

Probability of Picking a Vowel

The probability of picking a vowel is 8.

a. $\dfrac{1}{4}$, independent event

b. $\dfrac{1}{8}$, independent event

c. $\dfrac{3}{10}$, dependent event

d. $\dfrac{1}{6}$, dependent event.

Ariel Goes Shopping

a. $\dfrac{1}{12}$

b. $\dfrac{1}{6}$

Penny, Dime, and Nickel

a. 0

b. $\dfrac{1}{2}$

c. $\dfrac{3}{16}$

prepaze

Science Answer Key

Plant and Animal Cell

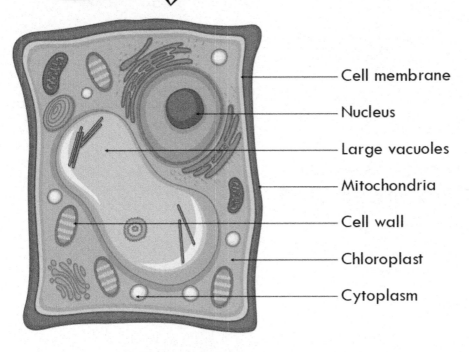

- Cell membrane
- Nucleus
- Large vacuoles
- Mitochondria
- Cell wall
- Chloroplast
- Cytoplasm

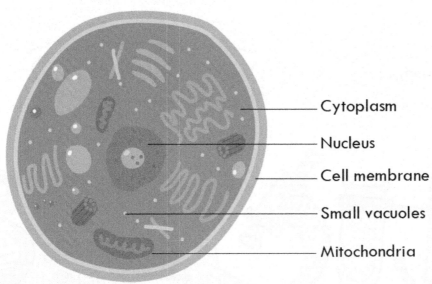

- Cytoplasm
- Nucleus
- Cell membrane
- Small vacuoles
- Mitochondria

Similarities between Plant and Animal Cell

Plant cell organelles	Common organelles	Animal cell organelles
Cell wall	Mitochondria	Small vacuoles
Large vacuoles	Cytoplasm	Flagella
Chloroplast	Cell membrane	Centrioles
	Nucleus	
	Golgi apparatus	
	Endoplasmic reticulum	

Types of cells

Eukaryotes Vs Prokaryotes

PROKARYOTE

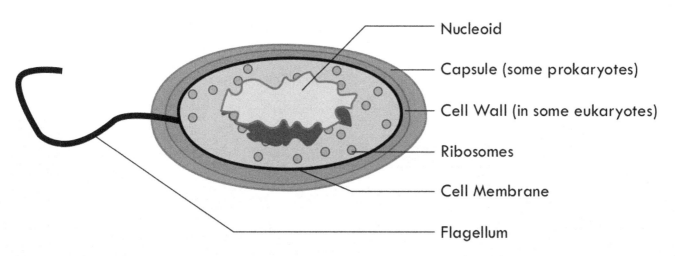

- Nucleoid
- Capsule (some prokaryotes)
- Cell Wall (in some eukaryotes)
- Ribosomes
- Cell Membrane
- Flagellum

EUKARYOTE

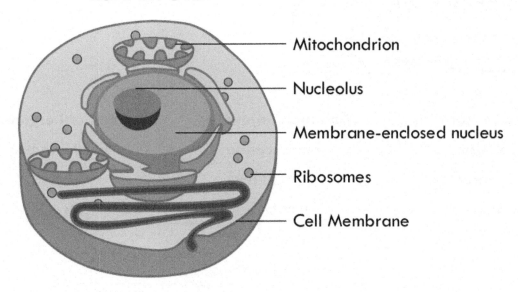

Mitochondrion

Nucleolus

Membrane-enclosed nucleus

Ribosomes

Cell Membrane

Eukaryote	Prokaryote
Membrane bound nucleus and nucleolus	Unbound nucleoid
Linear DNA with histones	Circular DNA
Membrane bound organelles are present	No membrane bound organelles are present
Some cells have a simple cell wall	Complex cell wall
Big ribosomes	Small ribosomes
Multicellular organisms	Unicellular organisms
Cell division by binary fission	Cell division by mitosis

No	organelles	functions
1	Cell membrane	provides shape and structure
2	Cell wall	controls cell functions
3	Flagella	makes lipids and proteins
4	Nucleus	stores water and substances
5	Ribosome	stores and controls movement of molecules made by the ER
6	Endoplasmic reticulum	regulates movement of substances in and out the cell
7	Mitochondria	helps in movement
8	Vacuole	produces protein
9	Chloroplast	releases energy
10	Golgi apparatus	makes food for the plant cell

Cellular Respiration – Crossword

Cell Division

Mitosis

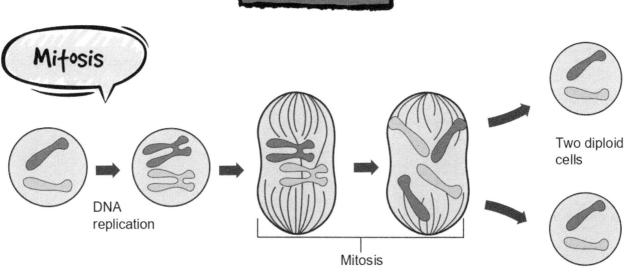

DNA
replication

Mitosis

Two diploid
cells

Stages of Mitosis

1.	E. Anaphase	10.	D. Metaphase
2.	B. Interphase	11.	A. Prophase
3.	C. Telophase	12.	B. Interphase
4.	C. Telophase	13.	B. Interphase
5.	C. Telophase	14.	C. Telophase
6.	D. Metaphase	15.	B. Interphase
7.	A. Prophase	16.	C. Telophase
8.	C. Telophase	17.	B. Interphase
9.	E. Anaphase	18.	D. Metaphase

Normal Cell Vs Cancerous Cell

Normal Cell	Cancerous Cell
The cytoplasm is large.	The cytoplasm is small
The cells have one nucleus each.	The cells have multiple nuclei each.
Each nucleus has a small nucleolus.	Each nucleus has multiple large nucleoli.
The chromatin is fine/smooth.	The chromatin is rough.

How Do Cells Obtain Energy?

1. Carbon dioxide

2. Alcohol molecules

3. Chloroplasts

4. Energy

5. Glucose

6. Cellular respiration

7. Photosynthesis

8. Fermentation

9. a. Mitochondria

b. Cellular respiration

c. Glucose and oxygen

d. Energy, water, and carbon dioxide

Genetics

Investigating Reproduction

1. Simply put, one generation of a bacteria is about 20 minutes while that of humans is 20 years. A similar comparison can be made with other organisms also.

2. This is mainly because human bodies are designed to produce only one type of gamete either male or female.

prepaze

Stages of Meiosis

Prophase I	Metaphase I	Anaphase I	Telophase I & cytokinesis

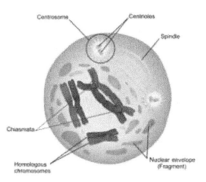 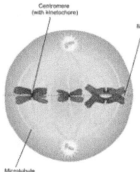 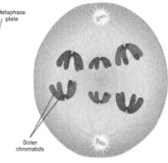 

The chromosomes condense, and the nuclear envelope breaks down. Crossing-over occurs.	Pairs of homologous chromosomes move to the equator of the cell.	Homologous chromosomes move to the opposite poles of the cell.	Chromosomes gather at the poles of the cells. The cytoplasm divides.

Prophase II	Metaphase II	Anaphase II	Telophase II & cytokinesis

A new spidle forms around the chromosomes.	Metaphase II chromosomes line up at the equator.	Centromeres divide. Chromatids move to the opposite poles of the cells.	A nuclear envelope forms around each set of chromosomes. The cytoplasm divides.

  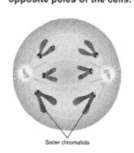 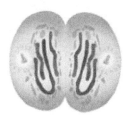

Mitosis Vs Meiosis in Humans

	Mitosis	Meiosis
Function	For growth, repair, and maintenance	To prevent doubling of chromosomes in the offspring
Types of cells that undergo this process	All body cells	Gametes
Location in the human body	Cell present in all parts of the body	Only in reproductive organs
Number of parent cells involved	1	1
Number of daughter cells produced	2 daughter cells	Male produces 4 sperm cells Female produces 1 egg
Size of daughter cells as compared to parent cells	Smaller than the parent	Sperm cells are much smaller than the egg
Change in the number of chromosomes	Diploid - 2n	Diploid - 2n
Number of divisions in the nucleus	1 division	2 consecutive divisions
Difference between the DNAs of mother cell and daughter cells	Daughter cells get correct number of chromosomes with a copy of information from the parent	After the first division, there are 2 daughter cells with half the number of chromosomes as that of the parent cell
Type of reproduction	Asexual reproduction	Sexual reproduction

prepaze

DNA

DNA Molecule

= Adenine

= Thymine

= Cytosine

= Guanine

= Phosphate backbone

DNA

Reinforcement: Genetics

a. Homozygous, because of the identical alleles

b. Heterozygous, because of the non-identical alleles

c. Homozygous, because of the identical alleles

d. Homozygous, because of the identical alleles

e. Heterozygous, because of the non-identical alleles

www.prepaze.com

345

prepaze

a. genetic, alleles

b. physical

c. homozygous, identical

d. heterozygous, non-identical

a. i. Tall

ii. Tall

iii. Short

b. i. Black

ii. Black

iii. Blonde

	T	T
T	TT	TT
t	Tt	tt

a. 75%

b. 25%

Monster Genetics

1. Blue-purple body color, horned ears

2. Blue eyes

3. Green body color, Clawed toes, Four fingers

Phenotype	Genotype(s)
Green body color	GG, Gg
Yellow body color	gg
Two eyes	EE, Ee
One eye	ee
No claws	cc
Five fingers	ff

	P	p
P	PP	Pp
p	Pp	pp

PP - purple

Pp - blue-purple

pp - blue

Branching Diagram

	Moosho		Dalo
	Jonte		Bobwob
	Bango		Jameson
	Floogle		Stricker

prepaze

Reading a cladogram

1. Curly antennae - F

2. Crushing mouthparts - G

3. Wings - D

4. 6 legs - C

5. Segmented body - A

6. Legs - B

7. Double set of wings - E

8. Cerci - H

Fact, Fiction, or Opinion

1. Fiction

2. Opinion

3. Fact

4. Fiction

5. Fiction

6. Fact

7. Fact

8. Opinion

9. Fiction

10. Fiction

Reinforcement: Evolution

Down:

1. Vestigial

2. Homologous

4. Speciation

6. Fossils

Across:

2. Hybrid

3. Flinches

5. Variation

7. Cladogram

8. Adaptations

9. Selection

prepaze

Rock cycle

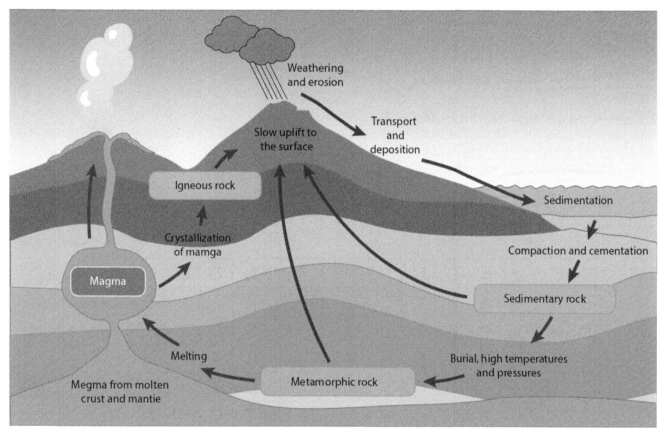

1. Rock cycle

2. It is false because each type of rock requires specific conditions to transform to a different type. For example, extensive heat and pressure changes sedimentary rocks into metamorphic rocks.

3. High temperature and pressure

4. Weathering, erosion and sedimentation

5. Crystallisation

Disturbed Rock Layers

1. Folding   2. Tilting   3. Faults   4. Intrusions

Sedimentary Layers – Puzzle

Order of layers from top to bottom - D, A, C, E, and B

Word Grid

B	T	J	K	C	M	N	N	K	W	N	G	B	Y	M
E	T	E	A	R	M	O	U	N	T	A	I	N	E	L
D	E	V	C	E	I	E	M	O	E	P	Q	T	Y	A
R	E	K	D	T	R	A	N	A	L	C	A	P	H	R
O	N	I	A	O	O	A	T	A	N	M	I	A	P	E
C	T	L	S	U	C	N	T	L	O	T	B	N	A	N
K	B	I	R	L	Q	E	I	R	E	F	L	G	R	I
A	O	T	O	T	S	H	P	C	G	D	C	E	G	M
N	S	V	L	X	T	H	T	M	A	G	M	A	O	T
O	O	U	F	E	I	L	E	R	O	C	P	R	P	S
A	A	C	O	C	R	E	I	C	A	L	G	I	O	U
F	V	Q	E	E	R	I	F	T	Y	E	A	D	T	R
I	G	A	Z	A	N	F	O	S	S	I	L	G	N	C
Z	D	W	L	I	N	G	L	I	O	S	N	E	D	P
Y	R	A	T	N	E	M	I	D	E	S	M	O	T	V

Vascular and Nonvascular Plants

Vascular Plants	Nonvascular Plants
Some have flowers or cones	Grow close to the ground
Have leaves, roots, and stem	Simplest of plants
Have a system of tubes that carry water and food	Must be near a source of water
Grow close to the ground	Don't have leaves, roots or stems

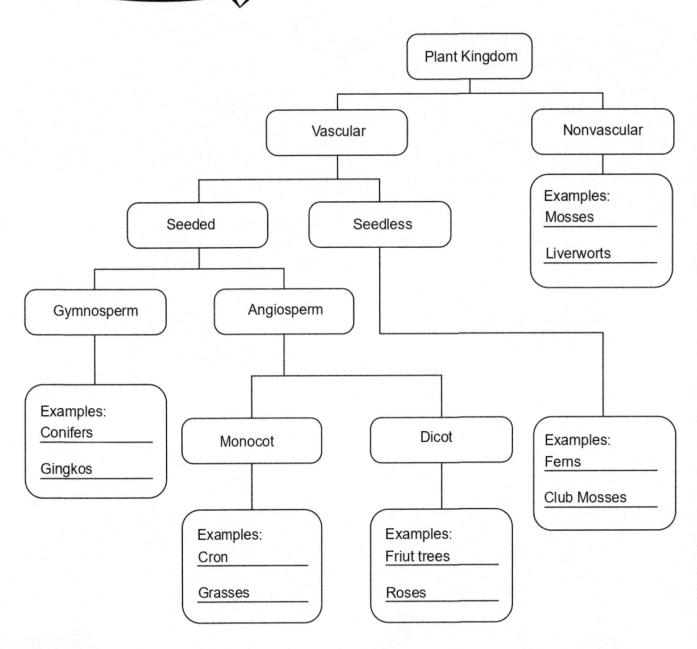

categorization of Plants

```
                          Plant Kingdom
                    ┌───────────┴───────────┐
                 Vascular                Nonvascular
          ┌─────────┴─────────┐        ┌──────────────┐
       Seeded             Seedless     │ Examples:    │
     ┌────┴────┐             │         │ Mosses       │
  Gymnosperm  Angiosperm     │         │              │
     │          │            │         │ Liverworts   │
┌─────────┐  ┌──┴──┐         │         └──────────────┘
│Examples:│  │     │    ┌────┴──────┐
│Conifers │ Monocot Dicot │Examples: │
│         │  │     │  │   │Ferns     │
│Gingkos  │  │     │  │   │          │
└─────────┘  │     │  │   │Club Mosses│
      ┌──────┴──┐ ┌┴──────┐ └─────────┘
      │Examples:│ │Examples:│
      │Cron     │ │Friut trees│
      │         │ │          │
      │Grasses  │ │Roses     │
      └─────────┘ └──────────┘
```

prepaze

Plant cell and Animal cell

1. Golgi

2. Nucleolus

3. Chloroplast

4. Cell membrane

5. Vacuole

6. Cell wall

7. Lysosome

8. Ribosome

9. Mitochondria

10. Nucleus

Parts of a flower

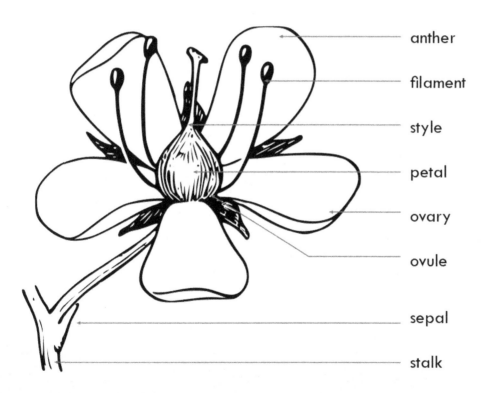

anther

filament

style

petal

ovary

ovule

sepal

stalk

Clues	Part of the Flower	Functions
I am the male part of the flower. Who am I?	stamen	produce pollen grains
I hold the anther up in a flower. Who am I?	filament	hold the anther close to the top of the pistil
I am the female part of the flower. Who am I?	pistil	sticks out beyond the stamen and lets insects brush up against it, enabling pollen transfer
I am the most colourful part of a flower. Who am I?	petals	attract pollinators
I produce pollen. Who am I?	anther	hold the pollen that contain sperm for reproduction
I am the part of the flower where fertilisation occurs. Who am I?	ovule	sends out pollen tube through the style to enable fertilisation
I am usually green and support the petals as they bloom. Who am I?	sepals	protect the flower as a bud
I am a tube-like structure that pollen travels through. Who am I?	style	enables fertilisation by being the location of pollen transfer through the pollen tubes

Seed Adaptations

Name of the plant	Image of the seed	Seed dispersal mechanism	Adaptations
coconut		ocean dispersal	The seed floats when its outer layers dry out. These buoyant coconuts can drift on ocean currents.
blackberry		animals excrete	Berries have attractive fruit pulp and small seeds that can be eaten by animals
dandelion		wind dispersal	The seeds are winged
burdock		animal dispersal	The seeds have hooks that get caught in the fur of mammals
green peas		explosion	The seeds are in a pod that rupture on maturity and disperse the seeds

Gestation in Animals

Animals	Gestation Period (in days)	Animals	Gestation Period (in days)
1. Dog	61 days	9. Zebra	370 days
2. Beaver	122 days	10. Cat	64 days
3. Giraffe	430 days	11. Chipmunk	31 days
4. Gorilla	260 days	12. African Elephant	645 days
5. Hamster	20 days	13. Guinea Pig	62 days
6. Moose	250 days	14. Kangaroo	42 days
7. Porcupine	210 days	15. Lion	108 days
8. Wolf	65 days	16. Human	266 days

Stages of foetal Development

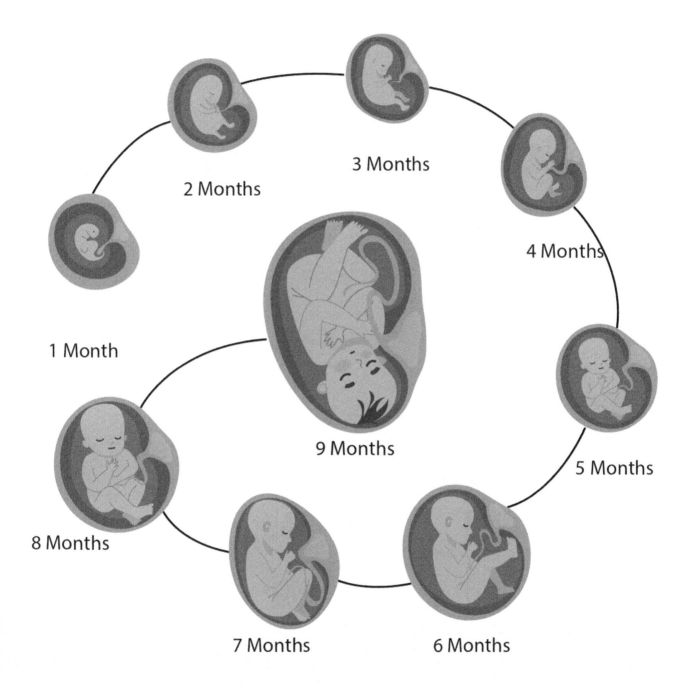

1 Month

2 Months

3 Months

4 Months

5 Months

6 Months

7 Months

8 Months

9 Months

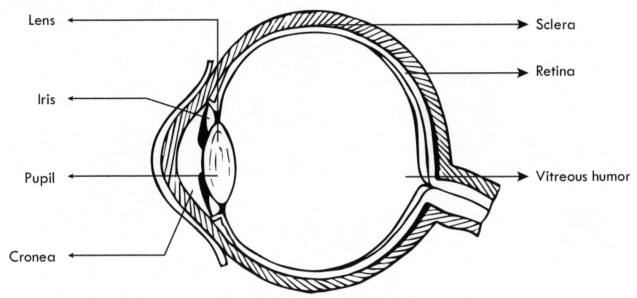

Lens

Iris

Pupil

Cronea

Sclera

Retina

Vitreous humor

Functions:

Sclera - provides protections

Lens - focuses the light rays passing through the eye

Retina - receive the light that is focussed by the lens

Iris - controls the diameter and size of the pupil

Pupil - opens to enable passage of light into the eye

Cornea - controls the entry of light, like a window

Vitreous humor - helps the eye to hold its spherical shape

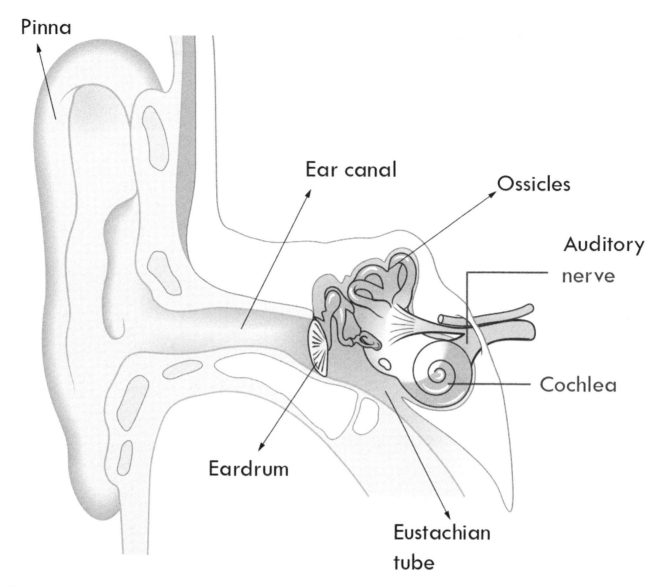

Pinna

Ear canal

Ossicles

Auditory nerve

Cochlea

Eardrum

Eustachian tube

Functions:

Pinna - acts like a funnel to direct sound to the inner ear

Ear canal - transmit sound to the eardrum

Auditory nerve - transfers auditory information from the cochlea to the brain

Eustachian tube - maintain pressure of the ear

Cochlea - transforms sound to neral message to be processed by the brain

Eardrum - vibrates when sound waves reach it

Ossicles - transmit sound from air to the cochlea

Physical Principles in Living Systems

Light Travels in a Straight Line

a. reached

b. did not reach

c. Light, straight

Systems in Our Body

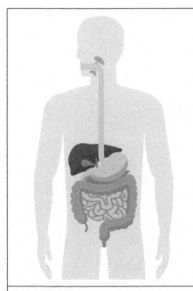	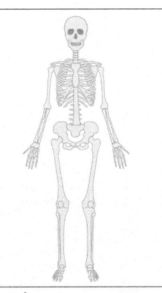	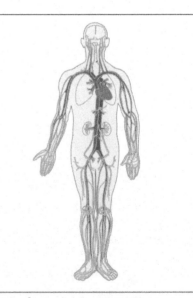
Digestive system	**Skeletal system**	**Circulatory system**
• Digestion • Absorption	• Support • Movement	• Transport oxygen, nutrients • Flow of blood

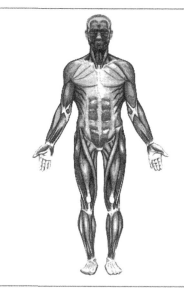

Muscular system
- Movement
- Provide stability to the body

Excretory system
- Elimination of waste products
- Maintain a balance of salt and water in the body

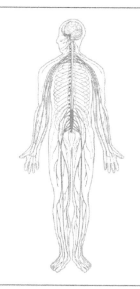

Nervous system
- Control
- Coordination

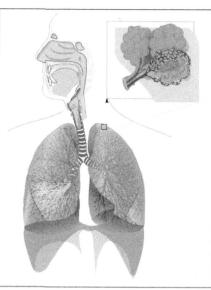

Respiratory system
- Exchange of gases
- Helps us with sense of smell

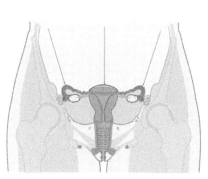

Female reproductive system
- Produce egg cells called ova
- Nurture developing offspring

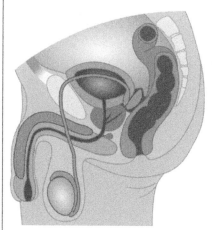

Male reproductive system
- Produce sperm cells
- Produce protective fluid called semen

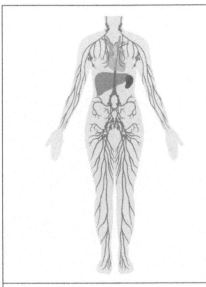	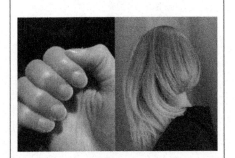	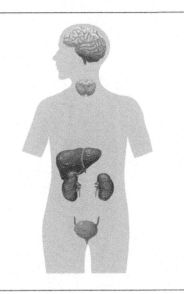
Lymphatic system	**Integumentary system**	**Endocrine system**
• Transports white blood cells • Absorbs and transports fatty acids and fats	• Protect body from outside world • Regulate body temperature	• Regulate blood pressure • Enable growth and development

Levers in the Human Body

First-class Lever	Third-class Lever	Second-class Lever
Third-class Lever	Third-class Lever	First-class Lever

1. Third-class Lever: the effort is in between the load and the fulcrum

2. Second-class Lever: the load is in between the effort and the fulcrum

3. First-class Lever: the fulcrum is in between the load and the effort

prepaze

Human Heart

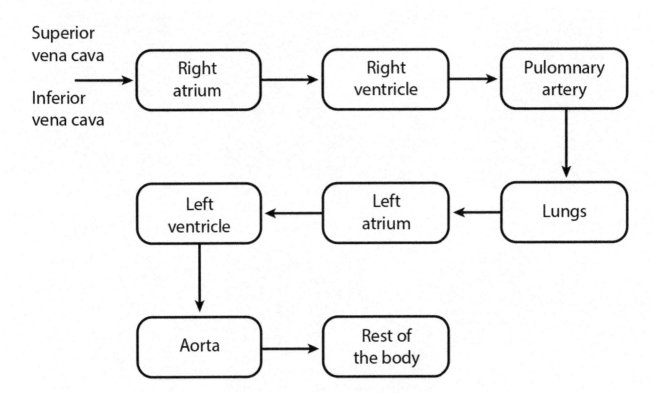

Superior
vena cava

Inferior
vena cava

Right atrium → Right ventricle → Pulomnary artery → Lungs → Left atrium → Left ventricle → Aorta → Rest of the body

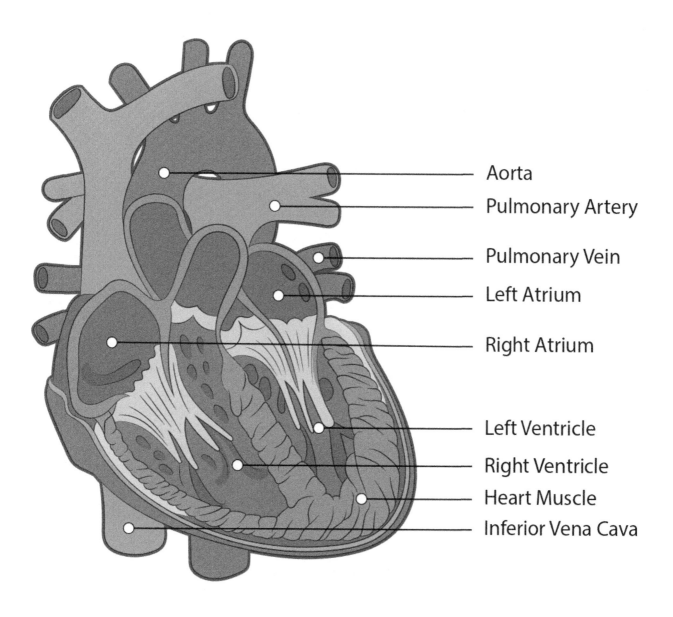

Aorta

Pulmonary Artery

Pulmonary Vein

Left Atrium

Right Atrium

Left Ventricle

Right Ventricle

Heart Muscle

Inferior Vena Cava

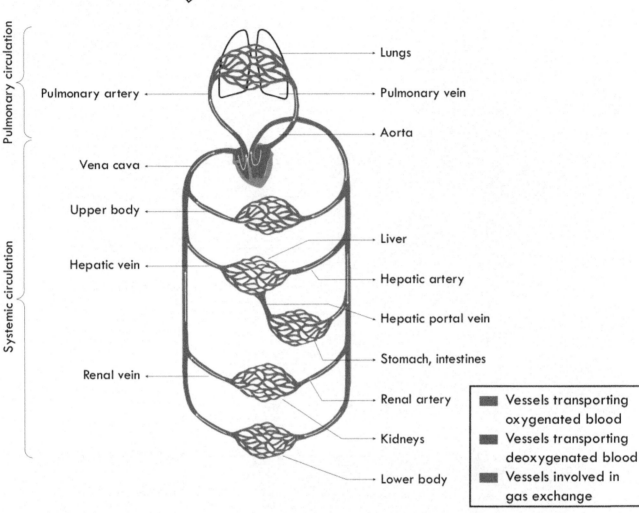

Pulmonary circulation

Systemic circulation

Pulmonary artery →

Vena cava →

Upper body →

Hepatic vein →

Renal vein →

→ Lungs

→ Pulmonary vein

→ Aorta

→ Liver

→ Hepatic artery

→ Hepatic portal vein

→ Stomach, intestines

→ Renal artery

→ Kidneys

→ Lower body

Vessels transporting oxygenated blood
Vessels transporting deoxygenated blood
Vessels involved in gas exchange

1. 4-5 litres

2. Red

3. Blue-red

4. Heart

5. Four

6. a. Left atrium

b. Right atrium

c. Left ventricle

d. Right ventricle

7. About 8 million

8. Valves

9. Haemoglobin

10. It is called a double circulatory system because the blood passes through the heart twice every circuit.

www.aceacademicpublishing.com

THE ONE BIG BOOK

GRADE 7

For English, Math, and Science

Ace Academic Publishing
ACHIEVING EXCELLENCE TOGETHER